ANTHROPOCENE

APOCALYPSE

BY

OPHER GOODWIN

Until All of us start to care for the planet, respect all living things and realize that we are all profoundly related from the simplest algal slime to the great blue whale we cannot truly call ourselves civilized.'

This book is dedicated to:

My good friend Bede – who might be a great cynic but, has a heart big enough to sink ships

My friends Dylan and Julia – whose sterling work caring for Fang, Hoppy and their friends is exemplary

My friends Kathy & Toby whose passion for Africa and wild animals and plants is inspirational

My friends Pete & Trudy who share my passion for nature and have motivated me beyond my bounds

My old lost buddies Tony Hum, Clive Hansell, Billy Mason and Jeff Bailey who I spent my childhood with

My wife Liz who wonders why I do this solitary obsessive writing and thinks it can't be good for me

My children and Grandchildren who I wish with all heart might inherit a world that is still as rich and marvelous as the world I grew up in

To all those who help build the positive zeitgeist and will save the wild things for ever!

Anthropocene Apocalypse

Index

The Blurb

For anybody who cares for nature this book is a must. This is written by somebody who loves animals in the wild and despairs at the degradation of the environment that he has witnessed first-hand in his life-time. You reel at the cruelty and thoughtlessness, the stupidity and crass superstition. You boggle at the numbers of this mad population explosion that is to blame. You can see the panic setting in as we career towards an inevitable human catastrophe.

Yet it is not all doom and gloom. The passion rips through your heart and the fury saddens you. But also in there is the ecstasy and love of the wonder that is this planet with its bountiful treasure-trove of nature.

We write so that it may not come true.

This book is not a mass of scientific facts or boggling information; it is one mans view from the vantage point of a long life of what is happening to this jewel of a planet.

It is also a book about hope; hope that we can use our intelligence to put a stop to this pollution and cruelty before it is too late. There are ways we can make it work. They are outlined. The way forward is clear.

All that is needed is the will to make it happen.

If you care about the planet you should read this. It will change your life. Hopefully it will also change the world for the better!

Anthropocene Apocalypse.

Introduction

The changes to the global environment have been phenomenal. The speed is colossal. The results are devastating.

It is only with the advent of the industrial revolution that the seeds of the Anthropocene epoch were sown. While mankind had been gradually increasing in number for some time it was the machine age that gave us the power to have a mass impact. The internal combustion engine opened up transport and suddenly the world was accessible. The huge strides in science and technology enabled us to conquer disease, predators and hostile environments. The Victorian age of exploration and discovery was surpassed by the modern age of exploitation and industrial utilization.

In the 20th Century we went from the horse and cart to the Space Shuttle. We now had the means and tools to get anywhere and cause change on a level unimaginable a hundred years before. The size of the population shot into outer space. The scale of the impact of urbanization, farming, mining, fishing and industrial activity was global and extensive.

To the Victorians the world was infinite. The jungles of the Dark Continent were impenetrable, the oceans immense and the air limitless. No matter how much you tried you could never have an impact on its enormity. That was to change. With the advent of industrial equipment the forests were easily demolished, the amount of waste from manufacturing was so huge that it rapidly began to impact on soil, air and water and the increased numbers of humans created more need for space and food. The infinite oceans and forests were suddenly extremely finite. The limitless land, sea and soil were unexpectedly found to be limited. Nature was encroached upon and all our systems became saturated with our effluent. We could no longer dump and pillage with impunity because the scale had become too big.

The Anthropocene was upon us. We had increased in both number and technology to the extent that we were hugely impacting on the global environment, altering ecosystems, creating mass extinctions, altering weather patterns and polluting the entire ecosystem. We were not only threatening the existence of our fellow creatures and plants but also our own future existence. Mankind had gone from minimal impact to the brink of global catastrophe in a mere hundred years.

The question that is now upon us is simple: do we use our intelligence to review the impact of the Anthropocene epoch on the planet and take steps to deal with the crisis or do we carry on blithely expanding as if there was no tomorrow?

It we continue there will be no tomorrow – at least not for us or a huge number of once prolific forms of wonderful exotic life such as the highly intelligent whale, dolphin and gorilla.

Personally I already mourn their demise. I fear we will destroy them and hundreds of thousands of other species. We will do this because we are caught up in a frenzy to consume and are unable to change to living in a sustainable manner.

I cannot see us having the desire to create a sustainable future. There are four reasons for this:

- The direction of society is controlled by a small number of hugely rich individuals who are extremely selfish and greedy. They promote growth and expansion regardless of the cost.

- The politicians, who control the world think only short-term, are motivated by power and controlled by the tiny wealthy elite.

- The vast majority of people have no interest in nature or its conservation. They see the bugs and insects as pests to be controlled and the gorillas as distant animals to be occasionally peered at in zoos or on nature programmes. They have little understanding of ecosystems and do not value nature. Their lives are consumed by the technological world they inhabit and they see it as divorced from the natural world. It comes as a shock to them when the air becomes unbreathable, their houses are flooded or they develop cancer as a result of a pollutant.

- The religious believe that God will sort it all out, that we were meant to have huge numbers of progeny and use the land as we see fit. Seemingly it was created for us to despoil.

There is insanity at work.

The next hundred years are crucial. When you look back to reflect upon the human world of a mere hundred years previous you can see it was a different world altogether. 'Progress' has not slowed down. In a hundred years time our modern world will seem just as archaic and primitive as that of our 19th century forebears. We will either have controlled our mad rush towards oblivion, and so have created a sustainable future, or we will no longer exist as a species.

It is a stark choice. The Anthropocene is upon us with all the impact of a comet!

My Worst Nightmare.

My worst nightmare is that we go on as we are. Our numbers steadily increase. Our life expectancy increases. We take more and more of the resources, room, and fertile land. We fill the air, land and sea with our waste. We chop down the forests, pollute the seas, and poison the atmosphere.

We end up with a world that is only full of human beings and the life we tolerate: our pets, gardens and benign wildlife.

There will be no room on our planet for wilderness, wild creatures and anything we term dangerous or a pest. Our rhinos will have all gone to superstitious Chinese medicine. Our elephants will only exist as ivory trinkets. Our dolphins, whales and porpoises will have been cruelly slaughtered for cat food. Our nearest relatives – the primates will have been hunted to extinction for bush-meat.

In my nightmare the forests are all gone. The seas are fished out pools of acidic stagnancy. There are no insects to pollinate the crops. There are no crops or livestock because mycoprotein is cheaper to produce on an industrial scale in humungous vats in factories. People are packed in to their allotted domiciles and the ecosystem is manufactured.

My Best Outcome

We limit our numbers and give half of the planet over to wilderness. We make room for the wild things and protect all the endangered species from becoming extinct. We educate the population not to resort to superstitious quackery, poaching or hunting. We maintain our forests and oceans, reduce our pollution through advanced technology, and conserve our resources.

Surely that cannot be too difficult for an intelligent species? Can it?

The most likely scenario

We continue blindly down the same path of unlimited growth and expansion. We make periodic limited gestures to deal with the various crises that are the direct result of our actions. We build flood barriers to deal with rising sea levels; we develop new farming techniques to produce more food; we introduce industrial food production from waste, we introduce cleaner energy supply; we put in limited conservation programmes and we deal with the wars and conflicts that result from the battle for diminishing resources.

It is an inadequate rearguard action that will have little real effect.

More forest is destroyed, more pollution is produced, the seas become over-fished, the species extinction is rapid, the population continues to expand and we head for the full-blooded nightmare.

A mutated virus (possibly a result of either pollutants or hunters butchering animals previously isolated in inaccessible regions of jungle) creates a global pandemic that totally wipes out human beings.

The Anthropocene concludes.

The long term effect of the Anthropocene

As with previous ecological catastrophes the ecosystem recovers. The mass extinctions open up new possibilities for evolution. If it had not been for the last disaster that wiped out 97% of species including the dinosaurs we would not have had the age of the mammals and we would never have evolved to create our own apocalypse.

I already prematurely greatly mourn the demise of such as the tiger, rhino, elephant, whale, gorillas, chimps and orangutans. They were innocents in the cruel game we play. I also mourn the huge possibility for an incredible opportunity that we threw away. I fear our greed, cruelty and selfishness are the seeds of both our success and downfall.

Given a million years or so, even if we degrade the system down to bacterial slime, the ecosystem will bounce back, different, but just as diverse and vital. There will be a whole new array of equally splendid creatures and plants beyond our imagination. Evolution works that way.

The Anthropocene will be an extremely short period – probably the shortest. A million or so years from now it is quite likely that a highly intelligent animal, totally unlike us, will be excavating the narrow strip of rock containing the bones, relics and artifacts of a once plentiful species of mammal – Homo sapiens – and theorizing on their likely demise in much the same way we have done with the ammonites and dinosaurs. I wonder if they will conclude that it was suicide?

The Decline in British Wildlife

I grew up in the Surrey in the South of England. Even as a young boy I was always out in the fields and ditches collecting caterpillars, snakes, slow-worms, lizards, frogs, newts, toads and stickle-backs. My earliest memory of my obsession with nature is of being three years old and playing with a group of older boys on some wasteland near my house. One of the big boys picked a twig off an oak tree and the twig began looping up his arm; it was a stick caterpillar. I remember being astounded and electrified. I wanted one. My father had to take me out to find one and I would not rest until I had one. Eventually we found a little geometrid looper caterpillar and I was satisfied. It went on from there. Every ditch was a treasure trove, every piece of corrugated iron a potential hoard of nature's riches.

My back garden was a menagerie. I not only had all my pets: the guinea pigs, rabbits, and a shed full of mice and hamsters. I also had a big pit that I'd dug with a pond and rocks. This is where I kept my frogs, toads, newts, lizards and slow-worms. I had a big aquarium for the grass snakes though. I'd learnt my lesson there. I once caught a great big three foot grass snake after a big tussle in which he'd tried to bite me, played dead and exuded foul smelling faeces on me, and released him into my pit. He promptly ate all the frogs and had somehow slithered out. I didn't make that mistake again. I kept my grass snakes separate.

I also had my pet crow Joey in my shed. He was very tame and knew a number of words. I taught him to fly. He lived with the 1500 multi-coloured mice, the twenty hamsters and assorted gerbils.

I had a roaring trade selling mice, hamsters, guinea pigs and stick insects to the local pet shop. I once made £25 by selling mice at six pence (2.5p) each to that pet shop. That's a lot of mice.

I remember lying on my back in meadows during the long sunny summer holidays. It was so peaceful and pleasant you were surrounded with the scent of loads of different wild flowers and the buzz of bees and a multitude of other insects.

My back garden was alive with insect life. All the daisies were festooned with multitudes of iridescent flower beetles. There were shield bugs, hover flies pretending to be wasps and a multitude of honey bees and bumble bees. The buddleias were alive with tumbling butterflies of all different colours. I collected nearly every species endemic to England in or around my house and up on the chalk downs.

One of my hobbies was collecting caterpillars and rearing them to adult butterflies and moths. My favourites were the Puss Moths, Hawk Moths and Drinker Moths. I had aquaria full of different types.

I had my work cut out gathering stale bread from the baker, outside leaves from the greengrocers and all sorts of leaves for the caterpillars. It was time consuming but incredible fun. They were my life. Back then we had no knowledge of pollution, pesticides or overpopulation. Nature was vibrant all around us and there was no hint that it was already terminally threatened.

As soon as Spring was upon us I would head off to the ponds with my mate Tony and we'd collect frog spawn and toad spawn to set up in our own ponds.

We'd wade up the ditches collecting red bellied stickle-backs.

We'd wade in ponds collecting great crested newts and palmate newts.

Every day we'd rush back excitedly and divvy up our captures.

That was my childhood. My playground was the natural world around me.

Now, as an adult, I always check the ditches as I walk past but I never see the darting stickle-backs. When I walk through the fields I don't hear the rustle of lizards. I lift up corrugated iron but I do not find the grass snakes, slow-worms and voles that used to abound.

When I lay in the meadows I rarely find the profusion of wild flowers and there is no buzz of bees or stridulation of grass-hoppers.

Across from my school, when I started teaching, was a site of special scientific interest – an SSI. There were fresh water springs with ponds and streams, a profusion of dragon-flies, damsel-flies, frogs, slow-worms, water-voles and countless other fresh-water life. The waters were crystal clear and teeming with invertebrates. That SSI is now a housing estate and the streams running through it are clogged with cans and litter with never a sight of a minnow or frog. The water no longer teems with insects. The voles are long gone.

Even more worrying is the fact that I travel hundreds of miles in my car and never have to wash the windscreen because of splattered insects. There are no smashed insect bodies stuck to my grill or bonnet. There are too few insects left. The world has changed. The profusion of nature is now a pale residue.

The ditches that once thronged with life are now sterile with stagnant water and clogged with water-weed.

I fear the pesticides have put pay to most of the insects, including honey bees, and the fertilizers have poisoned the waterways – at least those that are not buried under concrete.

The rich ecosystem I grew up with, that was itself merely an insipid shadow of the diverse wealth of the system that existed before we chopped down England's great forests, freed up the ponds and lakes from the otters and beavers, and hunted the stag, wild-boar, wolves and bears to extinction, is now a desert in which the vestiges of that abundance struggle to survive.

I don't hold out much hope for the future.

Extinction of species – Zambia and Zimbabwe

As I drove in the old beat-up pick-up truck through the outback of Africa I was vibrant with excitement and expectation. I was in Africa at last. It felt to me like going home. As a white skinned Englishman I was filled with wonder. There was something magical about Africa. This was the land we had sprung from. This was our home. Somewhere in my bones I felt it.

Long ago my black skinned ancestors had migrated out of Africa and wound up in Europe. Over tens of thousands of years they had adapted to the new environment with its cold temperate climate and weak sun. Mutations had created pale skin to enable us to produce vitamin D from sunlight. Gradually we had developed slightly different features. Now thousands of generations later I had returned to the land I had sprung from.

I have no idea why my ancestors chose to leave Africa. Perhaps they were driven out by hunger or perhaps it was merely their adventurous spirits wishing to explore. Maybe they were hunters who blindly followed the migrating herds. Who knows? Their story has not been properly told. They set up home in Europe and created towns, commerce, nations and a way of life that was totally different. What hardships, adventures and stories they must have had along the way. Now, at long last, after countless generations I felt like I was returning.

I had seen the films of Africa with its vast herds and rich diversity. I knew Zambia and Zimbabwe were not renowned for their wild-life in the way Kenya and South Africa were but I was expecting some signs of life. As we drove over the red soil along the rough tracks through the bush I was looking all around me hoping to catch sight of birds, reptiles and mammals. There had to at least be some monkeys, didn't there? I saw nothing.

Along the main route from Lusaka I saw men standing at intervals at the side of the road waving their hands up and down. I asked my friend Tobes what it meant. He told me they were indicating they had bush-meat for sale. I noticed the trucks heading back towards Lusaka had carcasses hanging on them. There were monkeys, chimps and various deer, antelope and hogs. Seemingly the logging companies had opened up the interior of the forests. The hunters went in behind and shot the animals. They sold their kill to the truck drivers who sold it on to the markets. You could buy any meat you wanted right the way to the most exotic and endangered.

I asked Tobes why there were no signs of life in the bush. He told me that the locals ate anything that moved.

Later in my visit I went to the local hospital. It was a terrible place where sick people lay on stained mattresses in a prefabricated ward. It was short of medicine and bedding. The doctors worked round the clock dealing with a huge influx of AIDS victims as well as every disease under the sun. They were unpaid for months and worked to a frazzle.

There was no food supplied for the patients. Their families were expected to provide and care for the sick people. Outside there was a big circular pit with a grill over it. It was a wood-fired barbeque that served as the cooking arrangement. The wood was collected from the surrounding forest and the food cooked by the patient's family.

A grandmother was cooking a meal for herself and her daughter who was sick in the hospital. The meal consisted of some corn meal which was bubbling in a pot and two tiny yellow birds the size of sparrows that the grandmother had caught that afternoon. They were being grilled whole without even having been plucked.

You cannot blame people for killing the wildlife if they are starving. We'd do the same. But the affect on the environment was obvious for all to see. They had reduced the rich spectrum of life to a shadow of its former self. The jungles were silent and nothing moved.

Extinction of species – Cambodia and Vietnam

Now is the time for your tears!

I could never imagine that I would ever get to visit Vietnam and Cambodia. During the sixties when the war was in full swing, the forests were being showered with the carcinogenic defoliant Agent Orange and the population was being carpet bombed I could never imagine it becoming a top tourist destination for the British and Americans. Surely the Vietnamese would not permit that? Yet it was a top tourist attraction and here I was. Here I was in the land of the Viet Cong and Khmer Rouge and Pol Pot's Killing Fields and things had moved on. Money talked.

My first experience in Cambodia was to chug up the tributary from Battambang to the great lake and on to Siem Reap. The river was rich with small fish and bird life. We saw kingfishers, herons, egrets and a host of other birds that I could not even identify. All along the side of the river were bamboo fish traps. There were multitudes of families with nets and further down, where the river was broader; there were huge rafts with great nets twenty foot square. The fish were tiny. They were harvested and crushed into fish-paste which was then sold in the markets.

Those tributaries were incredibly fecund but the scale of the fishing left me in no doubt that we were not witnessing a sustainable industry. There were too many people, too many traps, too many fish being caught and too much profit to be made. It had all the hallmarks of a short-term industry.

I could not help but wonder what I would find it I was to revisit in ten years time. I was sure the kingfishers and herons would be gone and probably most of the fishermen too. It was a way of life that had probably existed for centuries but it was being swamped by the sheer numbers of people.

My next experience was to travel by coach through the vast areas of paddy fields on the road to Phnom Penh. I noticed this array of sheets set up like sails in the fields and wondered what they were for. My guide explained that these were set up by the farmers. The grass-hoppers jumped into the sheets and were funneled down into a container at the bottom. The farmer would then harvest these and they would be fried and eaten as a good source of protein.

It reminded me of 'Snack Street' in Beijing. I had walked along this road with rows of stall all selling candied snacks on wooden barbeque sticks. There were grass-hoppers, scorpions, spiders, beetles, grubs, caterpillars and just about every type of insect you could imagine. There were even snakes and lizards. They had been coated with crystalline sugar and were bought and eaten as a delicacy.

That was fine in moderation but if you harvest and eat all the invertebrates you remove a layer from the food chain and those above have nothing to eat and die. The birds, lizards, shrews and frogs die. Then the snakes, buzzards, owls, eagles, foxes and weasels have nothing to eat and die. Then the tigers are starving. The whole intricate food-web crumbles.

Later on when we were in Vietnam we went on an expedition out into the jungle to see something of the extensive tunnel system constructed by the Viet Cong during the war with the Americans, in the jungle I was at least expecting to see some signs of life. It was barren. There were not even insects.

My guide explained to me that the Vietnamese people eat anything that moves.

It seemed to me that the whole of Cambodia and Vietnam had become impoverished in regard to its animals and was still being stripped of its wild life. The Killing Fields were aptly named and still in full swing.

Extinction of Species - North America

In 1971 I found myself sitting on a Greyhound bus travelling across America from the East Coast to the West Coast. We'd started off from Boston and headed up to Niagara Falls and into Canada, then around the Great Lakes before dropping back down to the great rolling plains of America's heartland.

We seemed to travel for days across the rolling plains. It was an unbroken ocean of wheat stretching as far as the eye could see, rippling in the winds in metachronal rhythm, as if it was a vast gentle ocean of lapping waves. It was late summer and the wheat was ripe and golden in the sunshine. At one point we came across a great line of huge monster combine harvesters endlessly churning their way through the corn with an army of trucks at their side as the seed was sprayed into them on the move. There was never a pause as one truck succeeded another as they rolled relentlessly on.

You could imagine them rolling through the day and night for weeks as they cut through that endless sea of wheat. It was staggering to contemplate. The whole plain was now one huge field of corn.

These were the plains that wagons had rolled over, American Indians had camped and hunted on and the mighty herds of buffalo had roamed endlessly in their nomadic search of grazing.

Those buffalo herds were enormous and were described by early pioneers as an endless sea of rising and falling buffalo like waves of fur stretching from horizon to horizon – and horizons don't get any bigger than on the American plains. In front of the herds were the lush green plains of the verdant MidAmerica. Behind them was bare trampled soil and nutrifying dung.

On the way back from the West Coast to the East Coast I fell into conversation with a young American Indian girl. She had been to see her grandfather. He had contacted her and informed her that his time was nearly up and he would like her to accompany him on his last farewells.

Together they rode around and visited all the places he had lived in the course of his life. He was saying goodbye to all the things he had loved, holding them in his mind for one last time and making his peace with the world.

When they got back to his cabin he dug up the precious artifacts that had been passed down to him and passed them on to his granddaughter. He had built the cabin himself. It was dug into a ridge so that the walls and ceiling were the soil of the land. Only the front wall was logs.

The artifacts had been buried in the centre of his cabin.

She showed me one of them. She told me that the others were too sacred to reveal to an outsider. The one she showed me was a big, heavy rounded rock. Around the centre was a big, deep, smooth groove.

I studied the rock and could not make head nor tail of it. She explained that it was a weapon for killing buffalo. The groove had been worn by loops of rawhide. A warrior would loop rawhide round the rock, ride alongside a buffalo, swing the rock around and around in a great circle and then bring it down on the buffalos head. The stunned buffalo would drop to his knees and the warrior would leap off his stallion and rush across and slit its throat.

I find that hard to imagine the bravery and prowess of those hunters. A buffalo is a huge beast. A stampeding herd would have been a terrifying sight. To ride into their midst and ride your horse with no saddle or reins, guiding it only with your knees, at full gallop twirling a heavy rock on a length of rawhide and bringing that down precisely on the right area of a buffaloes head required unimaginable skill, athleticism and bravery. One slip and you were under those hooves and trampled to death.

The American Indians were hunter gatherers living in the age-old tradition of mankind. Their philosophy was to move through the land without leaving so much as a footprint. It was a hard life. They lived hard and died young. There was no mercy shown. But they had a great respect for the land and the living things they hunted. There's was a truly sustainable life-style while their numbers remained low.

The buffalo was the centre of their nomadic existence. They ate its meat, dried the meat and mixed it with buffalo fat to create pemmican or in strips as jerky to last through times of shortage such as the harsh winter when hunting was impossible, used its bones for tools and ornaments, its bladder and stomach as water containers, hoofs for glue, skin for rawhide, and used its hide as clothing, bedding and to make their teepees. Even its dung was dried and used for fires. No part of the buffalo was wasted. They depended on the buffalo for their survival. They respected it.

The American government realized this dependency of the Indians on the buffalo and decided, in their great wisdom, that the best way of ridding themselves of the canker of the American Plains Indians was to deprive them of their livelihood. They set up a campaign to eradicate the buffalo. Bounties were paid for buffalo killed. Huge numbers of people went out shooting the great herds. Wagon-loads of huntsmen rode along in trains shooting the animals as they went along.

The bodies were left to rot on the plains. The vast herds were quickly whittled away and at one time the buffalo were down to remnants of a few hundred. The endless sea of buffalo herds of millions of beasts were consigned to history. It was the first campaign to eradicate a species.

In a matter of a few years the buffalo were all but extinct. Fortunately, due to conservation policies, and an old-fashioned nostalgia for the buffalo (strangely now adopted as a symbol of the Wild West as if the massacres of yesteryear had never happened) the buffalo has bred back up to sustainable numbers and once again roam the plains of places such as that of Yellowstone National Park.

The Passenger Pigeon was not so lucky. They were a bird so plentiful that they were probably the most common bird in the whole of America. They were supposed to have congregated in flocks of over five million.

When a flock flew over they would blacken the sky. What an amazing sight that must have been though we'll never have the pleasure of witnessing it.

Unfortunately they were seen as a pest. The farms were devastated by them and farmers were none too keen. When a flock descended on an area they would pick it clean like a swarm of locust.

The policy was to shoot them. They were hunted for fun. Hundreds of shooting clubs set about the pigeons for sport. Why shoot at clay pigeons when you could have the real thing for free? With-in a matter of years the flocks of millions were all gone and not one survivor lived on. The passenger pigeon was not as fortunate as the buffalo. It has gone forever.

Good things

As Liz reminded me there are lots of good things going on as regards the environment. It is not all despair and gloom.

We have many conservation bodies who are putting pressure on to protect our wild-life right round the globe and they are doing a great job.

There are all the environmental groups who are monitoring the crimes being committed, bearing witness to the atrocities and telling us. They do not let much get past them.

There are the recycling projects to take the pressure off landfill and retrieve as much as we can to assist our dwindling resources.

There are the renewable energy initiatives to create power that is not polluting or harmful to the environment.

There is the huge advance in technology to make our machines more efficient, effective and less wasteful.

There is a raft of better legislation and enforcement to prevent our industries polluting the atmosphere, fresh water, land and sea with toxins.

There is analysis of our food, air and water to check the levels of pesticides, heavy metals, carcinogens and radio-active isotopes.

There are some great educational awareness raising projects and materials.

There is a world-wide awareness of the issues concerning conservation, pollution and habitat loss

There are many campaigns to save specific organisms from extinction.

I do not decry these efforts. I do not belittle the good they are doing. They are very effective in their own areas.

I just do not think it is anywhere near enough to stop the inexorable degradation of the natural world around us. My own eyes have witnessed the extent of the problem and it is too extensive. These initiatives are scratching at the surface of the problem. What we need is a more fundamental form of action.

The damage being wrought on a global scale is primarily due to the huge increase in the numbers of human beings on this planet. That is what hits you straight between the eyes everywhere you go on this planet. The cities are burgeoning. The streets are teeming and nature is being consumed.

We need to limit our population to achieve a significant impact. I do not see the steps to bring that into force.

Deforestation and extinction – Peru

We flew out to see our friends John and Katherine with their son
John. They lived in Lima in Peru and had been on at us to visit them
for some time. We finally seized the opportunity.

As Lima was reputed to be not the greatest of experiences for an
extended visit we worked out an itinerary to see something of the
country. This involved some internal flights, train trips, boat trips
and coach. It was quite an experience and took a fair bit of planning.

We started off by heading for Puerto Maldonado which was
supposedly a city but looked more like a ramshackle town in the
Amazon rainforest.

I'd always wanted to get into a real rainforest and this was it, the real
thing and my first taste of South American jungle. We set off down
the river in a small boat as parrots flew overhead and a small family
group of capybara foraged along the water's edge. I was actually
heading up a tributary of the Amazon. It was amazing. I was so
excited I thought I was in paradise.

We got settled into our room on stilts. It only had two walls. On one
side was an open space that looked out into the jungle. The other was
an open space that looked in towards the centre of the camp. At night
you lay in your bed, safe and snug under your mosquito net and
listened to the thousand voices of the jungle denizens as the local
ecosystem gave full vent to its feelings and passions. At night it felt
as if you were surrounded by a million different animals ranging
from tiny to huge. They stridulated, croaked, whistled and roared as
they sought mates, protected territory, called to each other for social
cohesion, or simply yelled out for the sake of it. It was thrilling. I
was so excited that I could not sleep.

Insects and bats shot through our room and you felt you were in the
midst of it. It was exhilarating. You could hear insects exoskeletons

being crunched up in the jaws of predators invisibly all around you in the dark. I've no idea what sort of creatures they were.

Needless to say I did not feel the need to get up and visit the toilet until morning.

The morning eventually came and I spent a while before breakfast watching the weaver birds going in and out of their elaborately woven basket nests in the palm trees. The parrots squawked, insects stridulated and the air was hot and heavy with the electricity of life. Even the air smelt rich and fecund.

This was how things should be.

We walked down trails through the jungle marveling at the stilted trees that supposedly walked through the jungle. They actually did. They grew new stilts on one side and moved to the side in search of light. It was slow-motion walking.

Everywhere was the singing of fecundity. It the afternoon we paddled up the tributary to a lagoon, found huge bulbous hairy caterpillars in the trees, huge colourful red winged birds in the trees, caught piranhas and baby alligators and watched the sun set in a great orange glow just before it rained on us in a torrential tropical downpour and we were soaked. Fortunately it was warm, as warm as a bath even though it was now night and we did not mind being soaked.

We paddled back to the jetty and clambered out of the canoe – our guide shone his torch round to show us what was around. My heart stopped when he showed us these enormous long-legged spiders with eighteen inch span, straddled on the stone wall of the jetty. As we made our way back I made sure I did not go anywhere near any walls.

The next day we climbed a huge tower that took us above the canopy. I was able to look down on the most amazing sight as the heads of all those tall trees jostled with each other to reach the light. There were monkeys in the tops of the canopy calling and swinging around in search of fruit, mist drifting through and parrots flying in groups from tree to tree.

When we flew out of there I looked back down on the forest. It was incredible. It stretched on and on. Yet when I looked the other way there was endless desolation. The land was laid out in endless patchwork squares where thousands of square miles of jungle had been cleared. There were burning pyres on freshly cleared land, crops growing in new fields and a desolate, barren landscape stretching behind into the distance where the cleared land was no longer fertile and was now resembling the lunar surface. The desolation stretched over the hills as far as you could see. The jungle with all its myriad forms of life had been ripped apart.

My mind flitted through the thoughts of all the billions of plants and animals that had once lived there and the future inevitable soil erosion that was bound to follow and the joy I had been feeling evaporated into the smoky air.

I found myself leaving with a heavy heart.

When I looked out of that plane's window it felt as if I was looking into the future.

Road kill in Australia

Road kill in America and Australia is quite a different connotation to that of a squashed hedgehog in Britain.

In Australia you could be unlucky enough to have a full grown male grey kangaroo leap out of the gloom straight into the front of your vehicle. That would make mincemeat of you as well as the Kangaroo.

Long distance Lorries were fitted with special bull-bars to take the impact of kangaroos and other wild animals. They were just a hazard of driving. You smashed them out of the way and drove on. Nobody considered the effect on animal populations or the animals themselves. The toll was immense. Indeed some people even went out deliberately running the animals down as a sport. To many of the farmers the local fauna was considered vermin.

The toll on local populations of Australian fauna is formidable. Fast moving animals like wallaby, kangaroo, pademelon, and wombats might jump out at you unexpectedly but other species that were slower moving, like Tasmanian devils, koalas, snakes, lizards, echidnas and the like just got squashed crossing the road to get to a fresh habitat. Every day the roads are littered.

In the early days nobody cared. There were millions of the animals and they were a nuisance. What did it matter if a few were squished? Fortunately now people do care and signs are put up, drivers take more care.

Coming back from a music festival with Pete and Trudy we went through the back roads and travelled long distances on untarmaced roads. There were regular warnings including reports of how many koalas had been killed on that stretch alone in the past month. It was 28 that month. That seemed incredible to me. We'd been looking hard and had not found a single koala.

Koalas are getting rare. I was desperate to see one in the wild. Everywhere we went we all scanned the trees hoping to spot one. Pete and Trudy took us back down the coast from Melbourne camping in the bush for two weeks. We saw lots of other wild-life but even though we went out of our way to look for the elusive bears we never had a single sighting.

At one point we stopped at a fresh oyster farm set up at a big lake and were talking to one of the old-timers there who had lived in the areas for decades. There were signs all over telling people it was Koala country. The old guy told us that the koalas used to be common but he hadn't seen one for years.

I was beginning to give up hope particularly when, after two months, it was time to move on from Pete and Trudy's delightful place. Pete and Trudy were experts in the outback and if they could not find one then I figured we had no chance.

We flew up to Brisbane to stay with long lost relatives and they kindly hired a place out on Stradbrooke Island which was an idyllic place packed with wild-life, one of the high-lights for me was having a colony of fruit bats living right next door to where we were staying. In the day time it was amazing to see them all hanging from the trees in such great numbers with their little foxy faces, sparkling beady eyes and reddish brown coat. They were huge. At dusk and dawn they would take off in great swarms and they would fly all around with individual alighting in our back garden to suck nectar out of the profusion of yellow blossom on our bushes. I was able to sit on our verandah and see them right up close as they gripped the stems with their claws and clambered around greedily lapping up the nectar with their long tongues. I was amazed. That was not a sight you saw in England. People in Australia take it for granted to see great fruit bats in the skies above their cities. Nobody should take it for granted. They are wondrous creatures. I later found that there was a huge colony of them in the city in Cairns and I was fascinated by them. In the middle of the city with traffic all around they were going on with their life completely unconcerned and likewise the pedestrians walked by without so much as a second glance. They were part of the furniture.

The fruit bats are now being threatened. Lately people have been getting concerned about the bats spreading disease. The lyssa virus is the latest scare. Some people have been killing the bats or driving them away. It's a tragedy.

On the very last day of our stay we were driving round the island when Debbie pulled the car up sharp. She grinned at us and told us she had spotted something. Reversing back up the road she stopped by this great eucalyptus tree and pointed up triumphantly. There at the top, wedged in a suitable fork, was a beautiful koala. He peered down at us inquisitively as we grinned up at him.

Not quite all the koalas had been run over yet then?

Road kill in America

Where-ever there are fast cars travelling through habitats occupied by wild-life you are going to get animals killed. When those animals are getting fewer and fewer and the free habitat less and less the slaughter becomes even more important. It is a real problem that could result in the extinction of many animals.

It is good to see that many places have taken this seriously and fenced off motorways and highways so that wild-life cannot inadvertently jump out at fast moving traffic. In many areas culverts and special tunnels have been laid under roads to enable amphibians to get to their breeding grounds.

In America if you are unlucky enough to go round a bend and run into a bison, bear, elk or moose you are likely to come off worse but it is the toll on the smaller creatures that is of most concern.

Our next door neighbor Jean, when we lived in Downey, was a biology teacher. Every holiday we would set off with the kids for adventures round America. Jean and Ceil (her companion) had furnished our house with a huge great American fridge freezer that was big enough to get a car in (well almost).

On one occasion we returned from a trip deep into Mexico to find a great bundle stuck in our huge bottom drawer along with the ice-cream. It turned out to be a coyote. Jean had found it run over but intact and thought that her students would love to examine it up close. She'd brought it home and because her fridge was packed had slipped it into ours. I think she thought we might not notice.

The kids were a little wary of the ice-cream after that.

On another occasion Jean had stuffed a huge owl in there for her students to wonder at. It was enormous.

It just shows you the damage that is being wrought on the animal populations and the kind of animal that is falling victim to the road traffic. Our beleaguered animal populations are being systematically destroyed by our motor-cars.

Further adventures in Peru

We flew into Cusco from Peurto Maldonaldo and were up high in
the mountains where the air was thin. There were lots of local
women in with their children and accompanying llamas and lambs
all dressed up in their finest traditional knitted costumes complete
with flapped hats looking extremely colourful and eager to pose with
you for photos in exchange for a bit of cash.

We visited the hotel where my hero John Peel had tragically died
and then went to the centre of town where we dined on divine fresh
trout with garlic sauce in an upstairs restaurant overlooking the main
square with its impressive cathedral.

We headed off by train up on the incredible fertile high plain. The
steam train was a marvel of Victorian design with brass fitments,
comfy cushion seating and dark varnished wood. It zigzagged its
way up to the high plateau – the altiplano. I could not believe that it
was so fertile at such an altitude. But the fields spread out all
bursting with crops to the edges of the skirting snow covered peaks
all around. The farming methods looked fairly traditional with lots of
bullocks, donkeys and carts being deployed tended by people in
fairly traditional costume.

On the train we were shocked when a shaman in full knitted body
costume complete with mask shot out of the compartment and
startled us. He performed a ritual at the back of the train that
involved burning coca leaves. He was then joined by an amazing
female partner all dressed in colourful Peruvian costume and he
played guitar while she sang and cavorted through her repertoire of
traditional Peruvian songs.

The train took us to Aquas Calientes (named after the hot springs)
the small town at the base of the mountain. It was like an old
American Western town with hitching rails. The railway ran through
the centre and there were no fences. Children and people wandered

up and down the line with the dogs. It also served as the main street. Health and Safety hadn't been invented here yet. You sat and drank your beer and ate your meal on the wooden sidewalk at the side of the track.

Next day we set off on coach up the mountain and I peered out at the thick jungle on both sides. The trees hung with epiphytes and the animal life was profuse. It looked to me like good old jungle.

Arriving at Machu Picchu we rounded a huge rock to be confronted with the most amazing sight of the ruined buildings and terracing with the back-drop of the most incredible and famous characteristic peaks. It was breathtaking.

The people who lived there were self-sufficient. They had constructed extensive terracing for farming and probably also scavenged from the jungle. It had been a large community. But once again I was struck by size. In today's terms that community would not have been large. It would have been small. You cannot be self-sufficient with large numbers. You could not support huge numbers with that terracing.

The tourist trade was enormous. I wondered about the expansion and facilities and how long it had to remain like this?

Heading out of Lima to the Ballesteros Islands

Lima had an old colonial centre that was great and had not succumbed to the frequent earthquakes. John took me to his favourite bar to savour a delicious pork roll and draught beer. We stayed on for another beer or two. I don't remember too much about that though.

We headed out of Lima towards the town of Paracus and the boat to the Ballesteros Islands. On the way out of Lima we went via the coast road. The beach was used as the city tip. They did not believe in land-fill in Peru. The municipal garbage trucks merely drove down to the beach and dumped their contents on the edge of the water. The resulting mess was lapped by the sea and picked over by gulls, pelicans, rats and nobody knows what else. The sea was full of jetsam, garbage and waste. I was uncertain what toxins were being put into that ecosystem. There was building waste and industrial effluent all mixed in. The Peruvians had a very cavalier attitude to waste disposal and pollution. The thick smoggy air in Lima was testament to that.

The sea all along the coast was heaving with refuse, plastic and discoloured water all along to Paracus. Little of the rubbish was biodegradable. It wasn't merely that it was an eye-sore; it was the fact that this was going to be a health problem for marine organisms for decades to come. It had devastated the whole area.

It seemed crazy that so close to the incredible Ballesteros Islands, compared by some to the Galapagos, there should be such reckless and unpleasant activity. Lima was a huge city but it was poor. The population was going through the roof and they cut corners on everything, from the unfenced deep holes in the pavements that unsuspecting pedestrians could simply drop into, to the lack of legislation on industry and commerce. Life was cheap, the population was expanding rapidly and the environment was of no concern. Getting through the next day was all that was important.

On the boat we were away from the stink and appalling sight of the open rubbish dump of a beach. The sea seemed vast and pollution free except I knew that was not the case. The toxins would be building up in the food chains and the plastic would find its way into various animal guts.

The Ballesteros Islands were everything we had dreamed of. Overhead seabirds flew in huge V formations while seals and penguins basked on the rocks in huge numbers. We saw Boobies, Humboldt penguins, pelicans and masses of gulls. Big crabs clung to the rocks as the waves crashed in. The seas were a mass of fish and the feeding was good. It supported these huge communities.

It was a biologist's wonderland.

On the way back to port we passed close to the incredible Candelabra which was a massive figure etched into the sand by the Incas in the style of the Nazca Lines.

I could not help wondering if it was done for the same reason as with the Nazca Lines; to ward off the evil climate changed brought about by El Nino with its ensuing drought. I doubted that it was going to be enough to protect the area against the marine pollution and over-fishing that was probably heading their way as the population of Lima and around went off the chart.

The Nazca Line and Lake Titicaca experience

It is one thing to read about them and quite another to see them.

The Nazca lines were massive lines drawn into the desert plain by the Incas. There were all kinds of shapes of monkeys with long coiled tail, spider, humming bird, and a figure that looked rather like a modern day spaceman. Eric Von Daniken made a lot of it in support of contact with alien spacemen as they could only be seen from above. Modern archeologists believe that the Incas in desperation at the changed climate resulting in crop failure and mass starvation were trying to attract the attention of their gods. They spent their energy drawing out these vast shapes in the desert plains and sacrificing 'volunteers' who were probably promised eternal life. When the rains still did not come they drew more elaborate shapes and went into a frenzy of sacrifices. Perhaps they should have put their efforts into a more scientific approach?

As there were no gods, and still aren't, the climate continued to fail them and no amount of sacrifices or detailed lines in the sand made any difference. The Inca civilization collapsed.

Perhaps the Inca experience is a warning to us? Perhaps we need to put a bit more research into climate change so we can bring our resources to bear to prevent environmental catastrophes in the future?

We flew round the plain in a small aircraft, banking steeply first one way and then the other so that we got a good view. They were very clear from above and mind boggling but clearly no remedy for climate change. The rains still have not returned. The plains are arid and infertile. Once again religion and superstition fails us.

After the Nazca Lines it was back to Lima and off across the high plateau to Lake Titicaca. We had a look at the incredible floating islands with villages all made of reeds. The people greeted us in traditional garb and we went for a ride in their reed boats, ate reeds and looked at their cormorants. Then we headed off to the island in the lake and I've no doubt the reed island people packed up and went back to their home on the mainland for tea and to get out of their work clothes.

The island was much the same as the reed island had been in that it was beautiful and the locals all greeted us in traditional colourful knitted gear. Everywhere you went everyone was knitting. Even little kids were knitting. You could buy all the costumes, gloves and hats knitted from soft llama wool. There was a festival with much dancing. It was supposedly a very traditional dance dating way back to Inca times in which all the village, dressed in their greatest finery, playing on pan-pipes, beating drums and guitars, shuffled along in line in a great circle and then performed twirls and elaborate steps. It was interesting and impressive.

I was getting the strong impression that the whole world was fast becoming a Disney tourist experience. The archeological sites were constructed for tourists, the nature sights and places of interest all neatly presented.

Sadly I saw that the only real hope for the future of wild-life was to become a tourist trap. I could imagine the safari parks with turn-style entry and little pockets of 'the rainforest experience'.

Hello Mr. Rhino and Mrs. Elephant – it's all just a game – you feature in the survival show – if you generate enough cash you get to live!

The Colca Canyon and that Condor moment

In order to getting over the effects of altitude as we travelled on the train to the Colca Canyon we had to chew coca leaves. At least I chewed vast wads of the stuff and Liz drank hers sedately in tea. Seemingly you have to have a whole roomful of the leaves to get enough effective cocaine but it seemed to work. We forgot on the way back and both felt not too good.

We stopped at a little place called La Raya with its picturesque chapel and obligatory locals selling rugs, clothing and hats knitted or woven from Llama wool. The locals were all dressed up in local kit and looked extremely colourful.

La Raya was 4829 metres above sea level. That is over 11,000 feet. No wonder we needed the coca leaves!

There were these green plants that looked and felt like green boulders of rock. I haven't a clue what they were but they were extremely impressive.

We made our way across the altiplano.

The Colca Canyon was an incredible huge long canyon with great ancient terracing along its length all creating a pattern of differing hues.

At the end of the canyon we stopped for the tour de force – to experience that condor moment! The huge birds were all around. They came out as the sun got up to catch the thermals so that they could soar to great heights. Some perched quite close and others flew seemingly inches above your head. They were huge majestic birds and an immense tourist attraction. Thousands of tourists flocked to get their shots and see the incredible creatures. To see them close up and watch them take to the air and fly was indescribable. They were gigantic! It was a privilege to see them fly wild and free. But it reinforced my view of the way things were heading. If it made money it was allowed to live.

I knew this bunch of birds was going to be OK. They were certainly bringing the cash in and earning their keep!

On the way back we stopped at a town that was holding some sort of religious festival. This involved the same sort of shuffling dance and similar costumes that we had seen on the island in Lake Titicaca and also similar twirls and dance steps.

What particularly caught my eye were the three birds they had in tow. There were these three men standing with great birds of prey sitting on these big hats on their heads. The birds were two massive eagles and a condor that made the big eagles look tiny.

The guy with the condor on his head must have had neck muscles of steel. That bird was massive and must have weighed a ton.

The birds were tethered with leather thongs that the men held in their hands. I later found that Condors were regularly caught by locals and used in their religious rituals. They even used them for entertainment and pitted them against bulls in some unholy, primitive blood-sport.

I'm glad I got to see my condors live and wild even if I was standing with a great bunch of similar photo clicking tourists. I suppose if that is what it takes.............

Species Extinction - Tasmania

In the course of my travels we went to visit our friends Julia and Dylan in Tasmania. They took us all over and showed us all around the incredible island.

We climbed up into the mountains to look down at the unreal chalky blue waters of wine-glass bay. The waters changed to pale green in the shallows and terminated in beautiful, pristine white sand. It looked spectacular and we could appreciate why it was such a tourist attraction. You could get cruises there and even, ironically get to swim and play with the dolphins. We thought that it had been named wineglass bay simply because of its similarity in shape to a wineglass. Unfortunately this was not the case. The bay had a much darker history.

The early settlers found the bay was a perfect shape. They would drive large numbers of dolphins into the bay, get them into the shallows and slaughter them by the hundreds and thousands. They did this with gaffs and sharp knives, they cruelly stuck and held them with the gaff and sawed through their necks. The bay was turned red and frothy with their blood.

The bay was named wineglass bay not just because of its shape when looking down on it from the mountains the red blood would extend up to halfway making it resemble a glass of claret.

Fortunately that barbaric practice no longer occurs there. Dolphins are highly intelligent animals with a brain as big as a human, complicated behavior and language. They enjoy playing and interacting with humans. I am sure they must have been just as terrified and in as much agony as any human being as they were cruelly gaffed and had their head slowly sawn into with a knife like in some slow-motion Islamic Jihadist beheading. It is unimaginable.

Yet if you were to go to the present day Faeroe Islands you can still witness that same vicious butchery for real. They still do precisely that in exactly the same way. Without regard for the dolphin's intelligence or social groupings, they herd them into the shallows in a bay, gaff them and saw into their heads. The waters of the sea run red with their blood.

The Faeroe Islanders see it as a manhood test and relish it. The dolphin mass murder is a time of carnival and celebration. The whole town defiantly all turns out to cheer.

I think the days of such barbaric butchery and evil cruelty should be long gone. Those men are not men; they are cold-blooded desensitized scum. There should be no room for such cruel practice in the modern world.

As we travelled round the glorious island of Tasmania to visit wonderful places such as Cradle Mountain I was struck by the amount of road-kill. Along every road there were dead wallaby's, pademelon and bush-tail possum. Every day at dawn and dusk the animals come out to feed and get knocked down by traffic.

I searched for a Tasmanian Devil among the carnage but did not find one. I did not know if I felt happy or sad about that. They were often among the road-kill and that was probably my only chance to see one. They are becoming rare. The chances of seeing one in the wild was unlikely. Their numbers have been decimated by a rare type of cancer as well as a high mortality on the roads. The fact that there weren't any among the road kill was probably testament to the fact that there were not many left. It was something to lament rather than feel grateful for.

Julia and Dylan lived in a valley in the centre of Tasmania in an eco-friendly house they built themselves using straw-bale technology. It was fabulous. All the water was collected and recycled, electricity from solar and everything insulated - an amazing house. The place was in the middle of nowhere only accessible by fourteen miles of dirt-road. They had a big wood next to them and a lake. There were many platypuses in the lake though we never saw them. Dylan and Julia's task was to conserve it and the wild-life around.

That made for a life well spent.

They never drove at dawn or dusk unless it was absolutely essential. On their land they had everything – wallaby's, pademelon, kookaburras, and delightful little blue wagtails. Under the shed lived a large tiger snake. I was wandering around photographing things and I nearly trod on it. It was coiled up in the grass and I'd taken it for a hose-pipe. It slithered harmlessly away back to its underground nest under the shed. It was supposedly one of the three most deadly snakes in the world. We saw it around quite regularly. It was a big fully grown male but it never bothered us.

Julia and Dylan told us sadly that when the first moved in to their house, just a decade before, it was common to hear the howling of the Tasmanian Devils. They never heard them now.

Protecting the wild-life was like fighting a rearguard action. The attrition of road-kill and encroachment of humans was destroying habitat and reducing numbers inexorably. On top of that there was the terrible toll taken by feral packs of dogs and pet cats. The indigenous animal populations had no defense against the ferocious placental carnivores. The dogs - escaped work dogs and pets, roamed the land and created havoc with the defenceless pademelon, wallaby's and possum. Even the Tasmanian Devils were no match for them. Packs of feral dogs were devastating whole areas. They had to be hunted down and shot though it was hard doing that in the Tasmanian bush.

At night beautiful, placid little Tiddles transformed into a heartless single-minded hunter and set off on jaunts to kill for pleasure. She would tear apart whatever she could and be back curled up the next day as if cream wouldn't melt in her mouth. Tasmania and Australia was a cat's idea of heaven. There were helpless marsupials to slaughter by the dozen.

Except that soon there wouldn't be.

Deforestation – Britain & Europe

Britain used to be covered from one end to the other in forest. It's where all our tales of little folk, fairies and goblins come from. The forest was a dark and dangerous place. There were large carnivores like bears and wolves; there were dangerous wild-boar and stag. You could imagine all sorts of weird creatures and supernatural spirits. It fed the nightmares and imagination and went straight into folk-lore and superstition. We have a fear of the dark and the power of nature.

At the time of the battle of Hastings in 1066 King Harold marched his men 300 miles up to Stamford Bridge near York to defeat Harald Hardrada who had invaded from Scandinavia. They concluded that bloody battle and then marched 300 miles back to take on the Norman invasion at Battle near Hastings.

These soldiers did not travel on roads those six hundred miles. They travelled down trails through forest for the whole journey carrying their heavy armour and weapons. Despite all that they so nearly won. A little bit better discipline and Britain would now be a different place.

Over the ensuing years those forests that Harold had marched through were systematically chopped down to create clearings for farming, wood for buildings and carts and beams and planks for our great fleets of ships. The great warships of Britain were made from good British oak. To achieve that the great hundreds of years old oak trees of Britain were chopped down to make beams. Some of these great beams can still be seen in ships preserved in dock in London such as the Clipper the Cutty Sark and Nelson's great warship 'The Victory'. They can also be seen in the great halls of England propping up the roof. I recently went up into the roof at Beverley Minster and saw the great beams holding that edifice up. Where they can no longer be seen is in our forests. All we have left of our great forests are scant remnants of the deciduous trees that used to cover our land.

We destroyed them.

Along with the forest habitat went the fauna. What wasn't destroyed along with the destruction of its habitat and food web was hunted to extinction. The bears, wolves, beavers and wild-boar are no more. Most people do not even know that they were indigenous to Great Britain.

The landscape we take so much pride in – England's green and pleasant land – is a man-made creation. There are rolling hills where there was once dense forest. The richness and diversity of fauna and flora was decimated. What we have left is a fraction of what once was.

People were delighted the forests were cleared. They had land to farm and no danger from wild predators. It was a win win as far as they were concerned.

This was a pattern that was repeated right across Europe. The great European forests are now largely cultivated plantations of fast growing pine. These pine trees are a monoculture which does not suit many of our natural species of fauna. They prosper on mixed deciduous trees. The diversity has gone they cannot flourish. We are left with the vestiges and fossils.

It has created a moral problem for us. We can hardly criticize other countries for doing what we have done ourselves. If Brazil, Vietnam and Madagascar are decimating their forests who are we to criticise? We have already destroyed ours. It would surely be hypocritical.

We have to get over that. We did not know the damage we were doing back then. Now we do.

We have eradicated all our top predators. We've made it safe for people. These days the most harm you can come by in our forest is to be caught in the eye with a twig or to stub your foot on a hedgehog – and even the once abundant hedgehog is becoming an endangered species so there's less danger from that.

I may be insane but I miss the wolves and bears.

The China tiger

Our second visit to China was to see our daughter and her husband working in Shanghai.

I loved Chinese culture and food but was extremely upset by the attitude towards animals. They were brutal.

Arriving in Shanghai we went along the Bund to catch the sights. The Pearl Tower was impressive but the level of smog was high and it all looked hazy - too many people; too many cars; too many power stations; too much smoke.

We set off in the evening to eat and catch the feel of the city. Overlooking the Bund at night was wonderful and the Pearl Tower looked better all lit up. You couldn't see the smog.

We ended up in Snake Street. One side was now restaurants and night-clubs and the other was the snake restaurants. The blood from a live snake was supposed to give you vigour and the bile was meant to give you potency. In the past the men would visit the snake restaurant for their dose of snake blood and bile before heading off across the road to the bordellos for a night of debauchery. Some still do.

There were big glass aquaria full of live cobras. A man with a great flourish would retrieve one of the snakes with a pair of tongs and place it on a cushion for all to see. It reared up and opened its hood defensively. He then goaded it like a circus lion-tamer with a cushion getting it to strike repeatedly. Seemingly if it was angry it would provide more vigour to the person consuming its blood and bile.

Having got it riled he pinned its head down with a stick and clipped a heavy-duty clip on its mouth so that it was helpless.

He dangled it from a peg proudly as the snake writhed around. He grabbed its tongue, which was lolling out of its clamped mouth, and yanked it - laughing and playing to the crowd. It was a snake – something to be despised. When he was through tormenting it he took up a sharp knife, held the snake still and slit open its abdomen. He cut out its bile duct and plopped it in a small glass of clear spirit for someone to purchase and drink. He ripped out its heart and aorta and put blood into another glass of spirit for that same person.

The snake continued to writhe around in agony for a considerable time before finally subsiding into death. There were a row of them hanging up that had received similar fates.

Later that evening we avoided the shark's fin soup. We'd heard far too many tales about the treatment of sharks. They were caught with big hooks, wrestled on board where their fins were crudely hacked off with machetes and then they were thrown back over the side alive to flounder and die.

No thank you. I do not wish to be party to such barbarism. I will forego the shark's fin soup.

I looked around in the antique shops looking for a monkey table but I did not find one. It used to be common in Japan and China for the nobles in olden times to sample the delicacy of raw, living monkey brain. They had tables specially built for it. The monkey was caught. It was placed in a container under the table after having its head firmly clamped by special wooden cleaves. When the client was ready the skull of the monkey would be sawn off exposing the living brain. The diners would then participate of the living brain with special spoons, dipping the long spoons into the soft pink brain tissue and sipping it delicately. It was a most sophisticated thing to do.

I do not suppose the monkey appreciated the finer points of the refinement.

It was all nicely thought through and ritualized. It put me in mind of the same diligence and forethought applied to the shower rooms at Dachau where they gassed the Jews. The designers had cold-bloodedly built in windows so that the guards outside could watch the terror and death throes of the victims inside. It was a similar attention to detail and calculated application of technology. Human beings can be so cruel that I sometimes do not think we deserve to live.

We then headed off to Guilin with its incredible mountains. I used to think the Chinese Wedgwood designs were stylized until I saw those mountains and realized they were realistic. It is incredible how a civilization came be so sensitive, creative and elegant and yet contain such ritualized barbarity towards fellow creatures.

As part of our stay we were taken to a zoo.

The highlight of the tour was to visit the tiger, and I do mean visit. We were encouraged to go into the tiger cage with the keeper and sit on the tiger to have our photo taken. The tiger concerned was old, tatty and extremely fat, I had never seen such a fat beast, and not only that but he looked semi-comatose. I suspected he had been dosed with something. One of our party did go in to sit on it.

I did not take a photo. I found it degrading.

There were also pandas at the zoo and I went and had a look. I do not like zoos and the sight of the pandas left me cold. If I had glimpsed them in the wild I would have been ecstatic.

I find the experience of zoos depressing.

This is likely to be the only thing on offer to future generations though; their only opportunity to see our great beasts. They will see the remnants of the world's wild-life caged up in tiny enclosures, paraded as harmless with all the dignity of a prisoner serving a life sentence.

Britain in Shakespeare's time

Britain back in Shakespeare's day was not quite as nice as the plays might suggest. Life was hard and brutal. Life was cheap. You worked six days a week. On the Sunday you would go to church and then take the family out for some entertainment.

In London if there were no handy burnings, hanging or executions and there was nobody in the stocks to throw big stones at, smack with cudgels, punch or boot you might decide to take them across the river Thames, taking care not to fall in as it was a festering sewer, to the South bank where the entertainment business set up its empire.

Here you had a choice. There were the ubiquitous whore-houses and taverns or you could go to the Globe for a Shakespeare play, a comedy perhaps? Failing that you could go along to the cock-pit and bet on the cocks. They were trained with special razor sharp spurs on their legs. They'd be put in the ring to bet on and fought until one or other was killed. There was plenty blood and gore to cheer about.

If that did not take your fancy you could go to the bull-pit next door and bet on the fight there. It was probably more expensive and up-market. A bull would be chained up in the middle and ferocious, highly trained dogs set on it. The betting was always as fierce as the hounds. How many dogs would the bull kill before it was finally ripped apart and brought down? Our bull-dogs have a bit of an unpleasant past. They were specially bred for the task.

To vary the sport they might put a badger up against a dog or dog on dog. There were even bears chained up and set upon, though to make it fairer they did usually break the bear's paws first.

We always have been a cruel species. We are excited by pain. It interests and exhilarates us.

We've come a long way though. Those blood sports, which were ubiquitous across the whole world, are largely banned in most civilized countries. Even bull fighting has had its day. We still see various underworld thugs staging dog fights and cock fights and badger baiting but they are a tiny minority. Most people are shocked and disgusted by their savagery.

We have come a long way as a species. The question is have we come far enough? Do we have the capacity to respect all living things and their habitats enough to afford them room on our crowded planet? Or will we simply ease them out of the way and push them into zoos, museums and extinction?

Surely there's got to be room for wilderness, jungles, swamps, tigers, apes and rhinos? Surely we will not eradicate the elephant because they have big canine teeth that we can carve into ornaments? Will we?

I would like to believe that we can find a way to accommodate the whole panoply of living organisms on our planet.

Wales and the Brigands

I sometimes think that the road towards civilization is a race against time. Will we get there before our heinous vicious side with its greed and selfishness promotes our own extinction?

A long time back when our kids were teenagers we went to the beautiful green of the Welsh mountains for a holiday. We had our usual luck with the weather but fortunately we were in the car so the driving rain could not get at us.

With four kids and a dog crammed in a car with two adults it can become a little fraught.

We were driving around trying to take in some of the beauty of the magnificent landscape and find somewhere that might be suitable to get us out of the inclement weather when I spied a sign to an iron-age fort. Now I am rather partial to Neolithic and Iron Age artifacts and am always up for a shifty.

To the accompaniment of group moans of despair I set off up the mountain. At least, I argued, the dog should get out, stretch his legs and open his sphincters.

By the time we had got to the top the weather was considerably worse and this was July! The dog and I were the only volunteers eager to participate. The rain was coming horizontally and stinging your face. I ventured on and scaled the remaining part of the mountain until I'd reached the top.

The top of the mountain was a large plateau with a huge wall all around it and structures inside. The walls were six foot thick and ten feet high and made of slate. It was impressive. I stood at the top of the exposed mountain and the wind and rain buffeted me. It felt like a thousand needles smashing into your face as if you were being attacked by a manic acupuncturist. Even the dog looked as if he had had quite enough.

Down in the valley the fields looked verdant and fertile. The sun had come out and it looked idyllic. I couldn't help wondering why anyone would want to live up here on this harsh mountain top rather than down in that fertile sheltered valley.

When we got down the keeper, who lived in a little cottage by the car park, came out to speak to me. She told me that the fort had been made by carrying slate in big baskets on people's backs from a slate quarry twelve miles away.

That was even more impressive. To carry those loads up mountains for so far was almost unbelievable. I asked why anyone would want to go to so much trouble.

'Brigands' she explained.

Seemingly just when you'd done all the hard work and got the crop in the brigands would come along with their swords and jokes and take it all off your hands for free. They also liked to party, slay the men, rape the women and torture the odd person or two. They had a few favourite tricks like pouring molten lead down a funnel into your throat - or spread-eagling you. This entailed pegging you down, slicing you open from groin to throat and laying out all your organs and slicing them up, while you were still living, to create two wings. They obviously found this highly amusing.

I could see why people chose to live on mountain tops and carry thousands of tons of slates on their back to build defences. I think I would as well.

Those things don't happen now, thankfully. It shows what a long way we've come as a race. All that remains is that we continue to get better at dealing with each other, particularly people unlike ourselves, and start treating animals with the same empathy and compassion as we extend to each other.

Los Angeles smog and mountains

In 1979 we moved to Los Angeles for a year into a nice suburb called Downey. We had a big avocado tree and two orange trees in the back garden. Every day was fresh hand-picked orange juice. The estate was built in the midst of what used to be a huge orange orchard.

Los Angeles was fifty miles across and intersected with looping interstate highways. There were no pavements; you could not walk so everyone drove. Los Angeles was the city of the motor car.

I worked at the school which was 50% Chicano and had a number of gang kids from the Bloods and Crypts. Every night they would go out on their streets defending their 'turf' against the rival gangs. The death rate was quite staggering. I found the kids delightful. They seemed to keep their aggression for themselves. One of the kids took me round to show me what the graffiti meant. There were different styles. Some were roles of honour for the dead and some were lists of the people from the rival gang they went out hunting. They called these 'the soon to be dead'.

The gang mentality and idea of territoriality seemed to suggest a stress related disease caused by overcrowding. You saw a similar thing in rat and chimp populations.

Near the end of the year I got into a conversation with an old guy who lived at the top of our road. He had a big garden filled with huge melons, squash and cucumber. He told me that the thing he liked about Los Angeles was the changing seasons. He could have fooled me. Ever since we arrived it had been nothing but red hot with the exception of three weeks in January when it had rained.

I was teaching when it first rained and all my class piled out into the rain. It was the first rain they had seen for a year.

I went home and did a double-take. There were huge snow-capped mountains that seemed to come out of the back garden. We had lived there for six months and had not glimpsed them. They were hidden by the smog.

Los Angeles is in a big basin ringed by mountains. The mountains trap the air and the emissions from all the cars build up and the chemical soup is acted upon by the intense sunshine to form photo-chemical smog. It's dense; it's thick and it makes you sick!

To try to counter this there was legislation that all cars had to be fitted with catalytic converters to reduce harmful emissions. They obviously did not work well enough. The air was so thick you could cut it with a knife.

The way forward is to use electric cars or else small cars with incredibly efficient engines that sip petrol. But while fuel is cheap they will keep going for their gas guzzling chevvies.

It will come though. Technology is moving fast, oil is running short and getting pricier. The idea of burning fuel to create electricity and then using the electricity to power cars has two energy changing phases in which energy would be lost but with the far greater efficiency of modern power stations would probably be effective.

The Los Angeles air will one day be so pure you can see those mountains all year round! That'll be good for all our children's lungs, hearts and brains as well as all the plant and animals living in that great basin.

I have hope.

The Chinese experience

China has had a one child per family policy for some time in order to reduce their population though that has been recently relaxed. This is a policy that has been fraught with controversy with tales of forced abortions as late as eight months in, yet it is a policy that I applaud. Something drastic has to be done if humans are to survive on this planet and if nature has any chance of having some room. I cannot see how things could possibly improve without such a policy – though I think enforced late-stage abortions are a some-what draconian measure.

When I arrived in Beijing I breathed the air. It was smoggy. The previous armies of bikes of yesteryear had, due to the increasing affluence of the people, been replaced with cars and motorbikes. The air quality informed you that millions of motorized people were having an impact on air quality and it was not good.

The Chinese economy was flourishing. The Chinese people had buying power. They wanted what we had in Europe and who could blame them? They had Western style clothing and were all out of the Mao suits and into fashion clothes. All the big labels were evident in the stores. The shops were full of western merchandise. The young Chinese had their transport and night clubs. As you walked around the residential areas you saw all the myriad of air-conditioning units attached to the walls of their tiny apartments.

You could see the future. They would soon tire of those tiny apartments and be wanting nice houses. They'd trade their scooters and motorbikes in for cars.

There was a nice McDonalds on every street and it was all the rage. The trend was for beef and lots of it. You could forget your rice with a bit of chicken and fish. This was the new age.

Except where was the beef coming from? What forests were being cut down to feed the habit? How much methane would that produce? What was the carbon tariff?

It was chilling.

I bought Mao's little red book and started reading. Despite the one child per family policy the number of Chinese had risen to 1.1 billion.

At the start of Mao's book it stated that 'with a population of 603,000,000 it was impossible to move to proper communism. It had to be achieved in stages'. I did a double-take on the numbers. In 1967, when Mao's book had come out, the population of China was around 600,000,000. In the 40 years since then, with a strict one child per family policy, the population had almost doubled. And all of those Chinese were no longer content to have a simple peasant existence; they wanted full European/American extravagance with all the trimmings.

Just think of all the extra land to house them, the energy to supply their needs and the cows to provide the beef burgers. There was going to be a hell of a lot of extra farts. Those cows can generate a lot of methane and methane is a stronger greenhouse gas than carbon dioxide.

Things were hotting up.

The Forbidden City was incredible and harked back to a time when life was simpler but the rich still creamed off the bulk of what was on offer and left the crumbs for everyone else. While the average Chinese peasant lived in a shack with his pig the Emperor lived in sumptuous splendor with a multitude of palaces, gardens, jewels and servants. It was no wonder that there was a revolution.

The opulence and beauty of the Forbidden City was only almost matched by the lavish extravagance of the temples. They were incredible. The power of superstition was on show for all to be impressed by. That was its aim.

It was explained to us that the superhighway we were travelling on as we left Beijing was made from so many billion tons of concrete and the hardcore for the road was taken from the ancient city walls of Peking. They were proud of this. This was progress.

It was like putting a much needed ring road round York by knocking down the city wall and using it as hardcore.

You can't say the Chinese were big on sentiment.

The lack of sentiment was made more obvious when we boarded our boat to head off for the three gorges cruise down the Yangtze River. We were catching the last cruise before they flooded the whole thing. It was all part of the great plan - the great push forward. Without regard to the effect on the environment, potential earthquakes, ecosystems, or the families living and farming on the fertile land either side (Three whole cities had to be demolished and moved to higher ground) the river was to be damned and flooded. The hydroelectric power from a number of huge damns would provide cheap energy.

As we cruised along and took in the wonders of the gorges with its amazing mountains and rocks, some of which was shortly destined to be under water, we were told about the wonders of Mao.

This was the man who had ordered a fly tax. Every person had to present so many flies to the tax office in an attempt to cure the glut of flies. This was the man who made the people catch and kill all the birds because they ate the crops. You could say he was not too environmentally friendly. He was ignorant of the need for an ecosystem and the impact of his draconian policies. Without the flies the animals that predated on flies died. The flies came back in larger numbers with no predators to hold them in check. Without the birds to prey on the insect pests the crops were ravaged by pests and the people starved.

A little knowledge causes a lot of harm.

One of Mao's many stupidities was the virtual eradication of the beautiful Yangtze River dolphins. Once beloved by the people because of their gentle nature, intelligence and beautiful pink soft skin these dolphins were now nothing more than protein for the people.

Mao ordered that all boats going up or down the Yangtze should trail ropes with gaffs attached to spike the dolphins. Ten of thousands met a horrible death.

The Yangtze River dolphins are still hanging in there but are so rare that their future is looking grim.

Thank you Mr. Mao.

Modern man

The Anthropocene has just started. It is only with the huge increase in our numbers and our phenomenal expansion of technology that we have begun to have such an impact on the planet that we are rapidly altering its ecology and climate. Indeed most of the third world still lives very much as they have done for centuries. They have not yet fully grasped the modern technology. There is a further revolution that is bubbling under the surface bursting to erupt. When India, South America, Malaysia and China finally move into the machine age and people stop using their water buffalo and carts there will be a huge further impact on the planet.

This is incredible.

When all the Third World in Africa, Asia and South America aspire to having the same life-style as us the impact on the environment will be colossally increased – and that is without the predicted staggering increase in population.

Modern man has only been around for 200,000 years. That is the blink of an eye in terms of evolution. Even more incredible is the fact that the development of human language and culture is only a mere 50,000 years. We are not even out of childhood. Perhaps that is why we behave so childishly?

In such a short time we have gone from a small pack of apes living in the Rift Valley in Africa to a world-wide teeming mass of humanity that has spread from pole to pole and adapted to every climatic condition on Earth. That is phenomenally impressive.

In such a short space of time we have developed a range of cultures, races and attitudes. We have invented religion, art, music, politics, dance, textiles, cordon bleu, alcohol, science, education, technology and a host of languages. Our ability to imagine and invent is the key to our success.

If we are going to survive the Anthropocene and have an ecosystem worth a jot we are going to be calling on that imagination and invention big time.

Let us try it out.

Imagine the world of the future where there is no check on human population growth. Extrapolate it forward. Look at the huge numbers of people crammed into tiny compartments. Look at the urbanization as city merges into city and there is no space in between. Look at the loss of the entire natural environment. Look at the demise of all wild-life. Think of the energy required to operate those cities. Think of the food needed to feed those extra billions. Think of the demise of natural foods and the advent of factory produced gunk. Think of the pollution. Think of the oxygen producing plants replacing photosynthesis.

Rewind – think back to now when we have the opportunity to have a different future. See a world where population is controlled to sustainable levels; where nature is given 50% of the planet in which to thrive and be wild. Think of humans with space to grow and beauty to live in. Think of the diversity of the wilderness and room for all the incredible species that we could wonder at and appreciate.

Now look at what we need to invent right now:

- A global perspective and legislation

- A will to allow nature to exist and provide it with habitat

- A means of restricting our population down to a sustainable 5 billion

- An end to environment destruction and the development of a sustainable life-style

- An environmentally friendly source of energy

- A pollution-free technology

- Plentiful food without cruelty, pollution, over-fishing or over-farming

- A transport system that is not polluting and is energy efficient

- An equality of life for all humans

- An end to destructive wars and social division

- A system of valuing the enrichment the different cultures and religions we have invented have brought to human life tempered with a realization that we invented them and no longer need to be a slave to our social and tribal indoctrination. We can leave our social mores and religious superstition behind and move on.

You might think some of these things are not inventions; but they are. If we were to invent a way of valuing the richness and diversity of culture and religion but free ourselves from enslavement to the strictures those cultures and religions impose on us that would be a massive invention. It would remove grounds for conflict and war. It would free up creativity and enable humanity to move forward. Inventions can be ideas and philosophies as well as technologies.

It seems to me that after a mere 50,000 years we have arrived at a crossroads. We have a choice to make about the direction we head off in. We can either look up and plan which is the best way forward or we can put our heads down and keep forging ahead regardless of where it is heading.

I suggest we look carefully down both routes and select our path very carefully. The destinations are very different.

Deforestation in Tasmania

Tasmania is a beautiful Island. The flora and fauna are incredible with spectacular scenery such as Maria Island, Wineglass Bay, Devils Gullet and Cradle Mountain.

On the road to Cradle Mountain there were marvelous sculpted white skeletons of big trees all around. As we got closer there were more of them and it was noticeable that the other trees were not in a good state. I asked the warden at Cradle Mountain what was going on and he told me that it appeared to be either too dry conditions or acid rain. As the soil was thin it did not retain moisture and if the rain did not come regularly then the trees died. It was either that or acid rain from human activity and bush fires.

I had witnessed a similar condition up in the smoky mountains of Virginia where whole areas of hemlock pines were dead or in bad shape due to an adelgid (hemipteran) infection. Whole areas of trees were skeletons.

The Swedish and Norwegian forests and lakes were the biggest casualties of Acid Rain. The power stations in Britain were putting vast amounts of coal smoke into the air. This formed an aerosol of acids – mainly sulphurous acid (A less acidic acid to sulphuric acid) from the sulphur in the coal and carbonic acid from the carbon dioxide from combustion. This acidic aerosol crossed the North Sea and ended up being precipitated down on the Scandinavian lakes and forest. Ironically, due to the height of the chimneys and prevailing winds, Britain was relatively unaffected. The Scandinavian pines however were not so fortunate; they could not tolerate the acid and promptly died. Hundreds of thousands of acres of forest were destroyed. The acid also built up in the lakes and killed the fish. It was costly and disastrous to the Scandinavian ecosystem. It demonstrated quite clearly that pollution knows no national boundaries which is why we require global legislation, monitoring and enforcement.

I bet there were a few heated diplomatic exchanges. I bet no compensation was paid>

It highlights the need for an international body on pollution with teeth.

Dylan and Julia drove us round Tasmania. We stood at the top of the Devil's Gullet looking in wonder at the tremendous basalt rock formations a little reminiscent of the Devil's causeway in Ireland. The view was an incredible panorama. Tasmania is quite sparsely populated and the air is relatively pure. It was good to breathe.

We stood at the viewing point as the wind was channeled up from the valley and rushed up the cliffs so strongly that you could almost hang in it. It bowled you over.

On the way back Dylan and Julia stopped to show us the damage done by logging. All over Tasmania the logging companies had moved in and taken down vast swathes of forest leaving behind denuded hillsides with protruding stumps. The thin soil was already washing away leaving bare rock. It was heart-breaking to think of the animals and plants that were being senselessly sacrificed for a quick buck.

The wood was mainly eucalyptus and gum which was unsuitable for building as it buckled. It was being chopped down and bought up by China. The wood was simply pulped and would end up as paper and cardboard. The people were told it was good for the economy. It brought in employment and megabucks. But surely paper and cardboard can be made from recycled products or from sustainable plantations? Surely it does not require pristine Tasmanian and Australian forest? That is madness. That is greed and stupidity.

There was a deception at work to allay fears. Alongside the road the logging companies usually left a stand of trees. You thought you were driving through unspoilt forest but it was all a façade. Behind the stand they had ripped the heart out of the place. The landscape was barren and would likely never recover. The destruction of habitat was obscene.

Some people would sell their own grandmothers for a buck or two. Tasmania, Australia, Brazil, Peru, Madagascar, Borneo and Africa were selling their future. They were taking their children's heritage and selling it for short term profit, money into the hands of a few rich men. Not only that but they were destroying habitats, destroying all the wild-life and creating wastelands out of paradise.

It is so short-sighted – so stupid – so ignorant – so horrendous. When will it end? When there is nowhere for the wild-life to live?

What world will our grandchildren inherit?

Deforestation in Vietnam

Walking through Saigon is a scary experience. It teems with people. It is in a fast transition. Gone are the days of slender, waif-like girls in long tight silk dresses and large round raffia hats. Though there are some of these being deployed to attract Westerners into the clothing shops. Gone also are the days of roads full of bikes. These days the women are dressed in tight slacks and tops and everyone rides scooters and mopeds. Half the people wear face-masks and special colourful headscarves because of the smog and these have become a fashion accessory.

There are few places to cross the road and nobody stops at pedestrian crossing. You take a breath, step off the pavement and walk across the street at a steady pace; the motorbikes and scooters weave around you. It is scary.

The scooter has become the family saloon. It is not unusual to see a scooter with four people on it. A child stands at the front and holds the handlebars, the mother drives, behind her an older child holds a baby. Often the children are decked out in goggles or big sunglasses a headscarf and face-mask.

The scooters are used to carry goods and huge loads are piled on to them. You see a scooter go past festooned with large water-bottles, boxes or crates of live-stock. There was one with a full-size fridge precariously balanced on the back.

When the lights change it is like the start of an FI race. They roar off in formation like they were on a racing grid.

Yet for all this modernity there are still the old peasants coming into the city from the outlying villages to sell their wares with two baskets of produce suspended off a pole just like they have done for centuries. They squat on street corners selling their produce. It is a strange combination.

The markets are the same bustle as ever they were with fly covered fresh meat still quivering, sorry looking fish slithering around in bowls, various tools, sacks of different coloured rice and vegetables and fruits of all kinds. One stall sold paper products. When your love-one died you could provide them with what they needed on the other side. You simply bought a paper effigy of whatever you wanted, took it to the temple and burnt it. Seemingly it would materialize for them to use on the other side. The stall sold bundles of fake money, houses, motorbikes, cars and cameras. Amazingly they believed this! There was a brisk trade in paper goods and a mad throng burning the stuff at the temples. The smoke from the burning paper money and goods supposedly went up to the heavens where their loved ones now resided. All I could see was more smog and a contribution to the acid rain. But then I'm a cynical antitheist.

The worrying thing about the present Vietnam social situation is twofold:

Firstly – all those people riding scooters and motorbikes will soon be aspiring to drive cars.

Secondly – There seemed to be a huge number of young people with small children. We were looking at a looming disaster. That population was likely to zoom.

Those crowded, busy streets were soon to be even more jam-packed. The smog levels were due a hike, the housing needs would increase, the pollution levels rise, the pressure on the surrounding countryside increase and the over-fishing would take its toll on the rivers, lakes and oceans. The Vietnamese fishing fleet is currently the biggest in the world. A lot of the fish in our own supermarkets in Britain now comes from Vietnam. It looked destined to expand in a futile attempt to meet the growing needs of a burgeoning population and the export market. There was only ever going to be one outcome for that. There are only so many fish.

The future looked bleak to me.

During the Vietnamese War the forest along the 1500 mile length of Vietnam was so dense that the Americans could not see the Viet Cong movements. They could not accurately bomb their supply lines. They tried to get round this by foolishly dropping huge quantities of Agent Orange defoliant. This destroyed huge swathes of jungle and inadvertently slaughtered untold numbers of animals. They, along with the innocent farmers were considered collateral damage. Not only that – Agent Orange is carcinogenic and teratogenic. It had a terrible impact on the ordinary Vietnamese civilians that lasts for generations causing a large number of cancers and deformities in babies. If ever there was a war crime that was it.

If that war had been waged today they would not have needed that Agent Orange. Most of the luxuriant, tiger rich forest is gone. Since 1975 over 70% of the rainforest has been cleared. It has been largely planted with coffee plantations for export. The 30% that is left is under threat and dwindling by the minute. The government is in the hands of wealthy developers out to make a bigger fortune. Considerations of the future do not seem to come into the equation when money talks.

It illustrates the short-term thinking, money grabbing attitudes that presently run the world.

Someone somewhere has to come up with some better planning and one of them better be on population control!

The alteration to climate due to global warming

The build-up of greenhouse gases has gone on apace due to human activity.

These gases trap heat in the atmosphere and prevent it being radiated back out into space. Consequently the temperature of the Earth increases.

The level of the greenhouse gases carbon dioxide, methane and chlorofluorocarbons CFCs have built up considerably in the atmosphere following the industrial revolution. Carbon dioxide is produced from the burning of fossil fuels such as coal, oil and natural gas. It is also produced from burning wood, respiration and decay. The methane gas comes from the intestinal bacteria of ruminants such as cows, the draining of swamps and bogs and the decay in paddy fields. The chlorofluorocarbons are produced in many of our manufacturing processes such as the polystyrene of food packaging. As the human population increased we are busily draining more swamps, burning more forests, burning more fossil fuel for energy, producing more goods, herding more cattle and constructing more paddy fields.

The resultant carbon dioxide would normally be absorbed by green plants for photosynthesis. The major centres for photosynthetic activity are tropical rainforests and ocean algae. Unfortunately we have been chopping tropical rainforest down with gay abandon. A rate of 150,000 square kilometers is destroyed each and every year – that is an area the size of England and Wales every single year! As Roy Harper observed – 'This is like turning the oxygen off in the life-support unit'. We have also been dumping chemicals in the oceans which have interfered with algal blooms. We have seriously impaired the planet's ability to process the extra carbon dioxide. That is why the levels have risen. It is not any natural phenomenon;

it is due to human activity. That cannot be denied by anyone with half a brain.

The increase in carbon dioxide levels is having a huge effect on our oceans. The carbon dioxide is absorbed by the seawater and produces carbonic acid making the oceans more acidic. This is a weak acid but it has a detrimental effect on many organisms living in the sea – particularly those which produce calcareous shells. These include many of our corals, plankton and molluscs. The acidity is killing them.

Most of our oceans are effectively deserts. Nothing lives in them. The fertile areas are those areas around land, in shallow waters where light can penetrate. Fish need these areas to be fertile to provide the food for them to live. Coral reefs are particularly luxuriant which species rich habitats and great diversity. Unfortunately the shallow waters and coral reefs are among our most polluted and the ocean circulation is slow and takes decades if not centuries to disperse pollutants. Carbon dioxide is killing our coral. Fish require the food from the plankton and coral. The carbon dioxide is threatening this food chain.

I live in the North of England. The climate is temperate and the land is above sea level. It has not always been that way. It is easy to show, from the fossil evidence, that where I live was once under ice and at other times has been a shallow tropical sea. This is not because England has moved nearer or further away from the equator. It is not because the land has risen and fallen. The changes are due to climate change. The ice-caps have periodically melted or become bigger due to global warming or cooling resulting in raising and lowering the ocean levels.

In the last ice-age the first humans arrived in England though they would not have known it was there. There probably came hunting the woolly mammoth over the ice-sheet that extended right out to the

South of France. Those first human hunters walked three thousand feet about where my house now is sitting. They walked on a glacier that was thicker than our highest mountain. England was covered with ice and contiguous with the polar ice. The whole of the Vale of Pickering was scoured out by a huge glacier only a third of which was on land.

Along the coast near Whitby we can find a seam of shale full of ammonites. These organisms are cephalopods (similar to nautili and related to octopus and squid) who became extinct. They lived in warm shallow tropical water. The present position of my house would have been twenty meters under warm sea-water.

If all the ice at the poles were to melt the sea levels would rise by 21 meters. As most of our cities are at sea level this would be disastrous. Whole countries such as Holland would be at risk of disappearing.

In South America the whole great Inca civilization was brought to an end by climate change. The rain failed to come no matter how many Nazca lines they drew in the desert sands and how many gruesome sacrifices were made. The Gods did not come through. The rains stopped. The crops died and the people starved. It will happen again due to natural causes. That is bad enough. But it would be plain stupidity if it happened a few thousand years prematurely because we precipitated it. That's bonkers!

But it is not just the effects on climate that can be catastrophic, transforming jungle into desert or fertile land into scrubland, putting land under water or under ice. It is also the effect on weather.

Climate change produces great changes in weather patterns. Currents of air such as the Jet Stream are deflected. Currents in the Oceans, such as the El Nino effect are disrupted. This could mean the Gulf Stream alters course creating a more severe climate for Britain with freezing winters. All this could result in different weather patterns for different parts of the world. While the overall global effect might be one of warming certain regions might experience chilling. Some areas might experience exceptional rainfall and flooding while others experience drought.

The increased temperature also fuels weather systems that generate larger hurricanes, tornados, storms and cyclones. These result in huge devastation as we witnessed with New Orleans or the effects of the tornadoes in the Mid-West of America or they may result in exceptional dry conditions resulting in the sort of bush-fires we are seeing in Australia, Tasmania and California or exceptional rainfall resulting in flooding as we experienced in Britain during 2013.

These weather patterns are not normal. They are a direct result of global warming and consequently are going to get worse rather than better until we properly address the issues.

Human beings are small organisms living on the surface of a planet, like bacteria on bar of soap. They are delicate. The powers of nature can be terrifying. We have seen the devastating effects of hurricanes, flooding, droughts and extreme weather conditions on various parts of the world. If we do not deal with the warming effect of our actions on the global environment by reducing our carbon emissions and methane output we will find there is a lot more climatic disasters to come.

The argument against the global warming deniers

Incredibly there are still people who deny that there is any global warming or detrimental effect on the environment from human activity. They claim the things we are seeing are not due to man's activities but are a natural cycle of events. They are simply wrong.

The evidence is clear. There has been an increase of temperatures on a world-wide basis. The evidence is in from global temperature records, ice thickness measurements and sea temperatures as recorded by our new satellite monitoring systems. The information coming through is dire. It will vary though. Likewise the carbon dioxide levels and methane levels are rising. The forests are being cut down. The ocean algae are declining. Yet the deniers still argue that it is not due to human activity.

They are wrong. Scientific measurements are objective. They do not lie.

The deniers need to face up to the consequence of a runaway greenhouse effect. You do not have to go any further that Venus to see that. Venus has a surface temperature of 464 degrees Celsius. As water boils at 100 degrees Celsius all the oceans have boiled away and the planet has a permanent thick cloud layer. This is due to extremely high levels of greenhouse gases, such as carbon dioxide in the atmosphere. It is conceivable that the Earth could have the same fate if things really got out of hand.

Human impact is undeniable, catastrophic and unsustainable. If it continues we might even start to find oxygen levels declining. Now that would start to cause a sharp intake of breath!

We are very adaptable as a species which is one of the reasons for our great success. We have been here before. The climate has changed due to natural changes. This is probably related to solar output. The result is tropical and ice-ages. The global warming deniers hide behind these natural occurrences to claim that there is no human impact on the climate. They live in a fantasy world. The measurements are conclusive that we are affecting the composition of the atmosphere in a substantial way and this will impact on climate. The computer modeling demonstrates this quite clearly.

Incredibly, and thankfully, the ecosystem of this planet tends to create equilibrium. If more carbon dioxide is produced the green plants photosynthesise more and keep the level down. Unfortunately our activities and number are not only creating enormous quantities of extra carbon dioxide but we are also destroying green plants at an alarming rate and reducing the planet's ability to process the extra carbon dioxide. At some point the equilibrium will be broken and there will be a big shift with calamitous results. Once the point where the buffering breaks down is reached the effects are likely to be pronounced.

Overpopulation

Overpopulation is the biggest catastrophe facing the planet. Now that we have destroyed nearly all our natural predators, solved our food and water problems, managed to colonise the whole planet from pole to pole, and successfully mastered most diseases we are free of all population restrictions. Our population is now busy spiralling out of control.
We are now staggeringly over seven billion and counting. By 2050 it will be around 10 billion.

The human brain is a wondrous computer but it is still not capable of understanding large numbers. Those size numbers have no meaning to us. A million is beyond our comprehension. A billion is almost the same to us as a million. I can assure you it is not. A billion is a thousand times bigger! This is why people, including me and indeed all the greatest scientists and thinkers, have such a hard time understanding concepts such as evolution, cosmic proportions and the Big Bang. The time and distance scales are beyond our ability to comprehend. Our brains cannot grasp them. We cannot really understand the enormity of such large numbers.

Let us attempt to put that stupendously large number into some kind of form that our puny minds can make an attempt to understand.

Ten thousand years ago the world population of human beings was probably around
a mere 5,000,000 (5 million).

Two thousand years ago (around Biblical times) it had risen to around 200,000,000 - 200 million (due to the invention of farming, primitive technology and primitive medicine).

By 1650 it had probably reached half a billion – 500,000,000 (due to better technology and farming)

By around 1800 it had risen to a billion 1,000,000,000.

After the industrial revolution, with the incredible range of technology and the internal combustion engine, our population has gone completely out of control.

In 2014 it has topped seven billion – 7,000,000,000

By around 2050 it will have passed 10 billion – 10,000,000,000. That means that in what will be a mere thirty six years we will have added fifteen times the whole population of the world as it was in Biblical times to what is already virtually unsustainable for us let alone the impact on our natural world.

It does not take a great intelligence or much imagination to see that this is simply not something that can keep going on without having a massive effect on us, wild-life and the planet.

Let us look at that in a table to visualise it better.

Time	Population
8000 BC	5,000,000
1 AD	200,000,000
1650 AD	500,000,000
1800 AD	1,000,000,000
2014 AD	7,200,000,000
2050 AD	10,000,000,000

Or a more detailed table based on an average of the best estimates (note – the time is not evenly spaced):

Time	Population of the world	Increase in population
1 AD	200,000,000	
500 AD	210,000,000	10,000,000 - in 500 years
1000 AD	280,000,000	70,000,000 - in 500 years
1500 AD	450,000,000	170,000,000 - in 500 years
1750 AD	750,000,000	300,000,000 - in 250 years
1800 AD	900,000,000	150,000,000 - in 250 years
1820 AD	1,000,000,000	100,000,000 - in 20 years
1850 AD	1,250,000,000	250,000,000 - in 30 years
1900 AD	1,750,000,000	500,000,000 - in 50 years
1950 AD	2,500,000,000	750,000,000 - in 50 years
1960 AD	3,000,000,000	500,000,000 - in 10 years
1970 AD	3,700,000,000	700,000,000 - in 10 years
1980 AD	4,400,000,000	700,000,000 - in 10 years
1990 AD	5,300,000,000	900,000,000 - in 10 years
2000 AD	6,000,000,000	700,000,000 - in 10 years
2010 AD	6,800,000,000	800,000,000 - in 10 years
2014 AD	7,200,000,000	400,000,000 - in 4 years
2050 AD	10,000,000,000	2,800,000,000 - in 36 years

This is best appreciated as a graph:

Graph showing the human population of the planet Earth

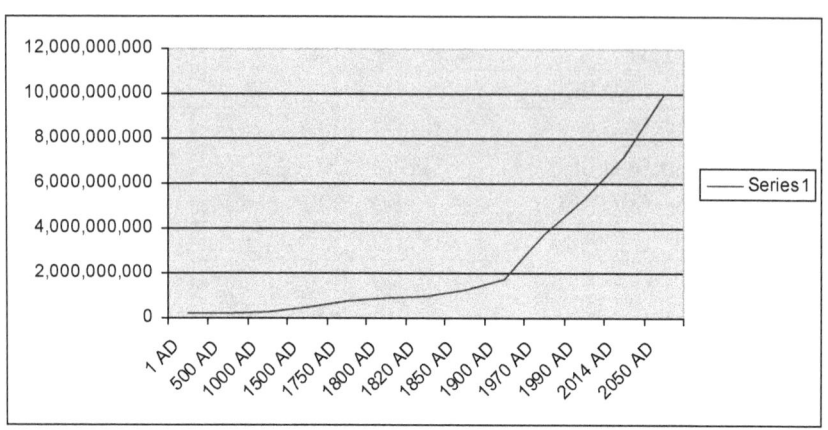

Please note – the time on this graph is not evenly spaced which might create a false impression. For the first thousand years there was barely any increase in world population. From 1900 onwards the graph shoots through the roof. The trend is for the graph to get steeper and steeper.

The religious among us are deliriously happy about this. They believe the world was created for us to use up and that this approaching apocalypse is a great thing as it is god's plan.
I, as an antitheist, do not share their rapture.
I believe that it is a catastrophe that is best avoided.

In all Biological studies of population increase a rapid rise of this nature is either followed by a catastrophic crash due to disease, lack of space, the build up of wastes or lack of food or a reduction in population to a sustainable level in harmony with its environment. The implications are obvious; either we reduce and limit our population or we will suffer a collapse of our numbers that may be terminal.

I would prefer that we applied intelligence and foresight to prevent a future disaster. I want my grandchildren to have a future!

It is the huge population increase that is largely responsible for the degradation of the planet. Because of the immense numbers of human beings on the planet we are:

- Taking over all available space and destroying the natural habitats in the process

- Polluting our environment with a wide range of rubbish, toxins and sewage

- Eating our way through every edible species on the planet

- Altering the climate dramatically

- Using up all available finite resources as if there was no tomorrow

- Annihilating species at a rate that has not been seen since the last major extinction created when a comet collided with our planet and put an end to the age of the dinosaurs.

The anthropocene (the age of man) has already been a disaster for many other forms of life on this planet. It is teetering on the edge of becoming catastrophic for everything, ourselves included.

If it continues at its present rate the ecosystem that has taken billions of years to evolve will be irreparably destroyed. The climate will be altered and life as we know it will cease.

DNA will not care. It never puts all its eggs in a billion baskets. Whatever organisms are left in our wake will evolve to fill all the available niches just as it has done at least three times before when other catastrophe's destroyed over 97% of the species on this green jewel of a planet. It is just that we will not be around to see it. We will only exist as fossils in a thin strip of rock that future scientists, of a totally new species, will speculate over. Neither will all the myriad life around us be there to tell the story. This planet will be populated by an entirely new range of organisms. It will have similarities but be totally different.

I find that sad about that because I am quite sentimental and attached to both humans as a species and the ecosystem we inhabit. That future ecosystem might be just as spectacular but it will not be mine.

So what do we need to do? We have amply demonstrated that we have the intelligence and capability to conquer adversity. Can we defeat this monster of a crisis?

The developed world already has a zero growth in most instances. It is the economically undeveloped world, usually described as the Third World, which shows the biggest increase in numbers. It is still not unusual for people in Third World countries to have twelve or more children. This used to be the case in Britain a couple of hundred years ago but nowadays it is almost unheard of. The question is can we alter this pattern in the undeveloped countries?

Then there is the need not only to stabilise our population but to substantially reduce it here in the developed world as well. Can that be achieved?

Well as a biologist the simple answer is yes. We have all the knowledge and tools we need. We understand human reproduction and have the means to control our fertility. With good education and the application of contraceptive methods we can limit our numbers to any figure we choose.

In practice this is not as simple as that. The undeveloped countries present a number of obstacles.

Firstly there are many social situations to address before we are able to put this into practice. People have large families because of a number of factors. These include the following:

- Disease still kills many of the Third World children

- There is no social welfare to support the family in times of illness

- There is no pension scheme for when people get old

They rely on their large families to address these issues and needs.

When these social issues are addressed we remove the imperative for having many children. They are no longer needed to support the family in times of crisis.

Secondly there are the economic considerations. The world presently runs on a capitalist system based on greed and power. The wealthy exploit the poor. They require cheap labour and open markets. It pays to have a third world teetering on the edge of survival, willing to work and produce for next to nothing, with a huge repository of excess people to provide a thriving labour market.

There has to be a better, fairer, global economic system to create stability and enable us to exist without continual growth and need for more and more profits.

Thirdly there are the political situations. Politicians seek power and status. They think short term and are willing to sacrifice land, the environment and people in the pursuit of that status and power. Theirs is the business of persuading people to support them in war, strife and xenophobia in the name of patriotism, nationalism and glory.

There needs to be more global long term planning.

Fourthly there is the religious element. Religions vie with each other for power to give themselves credibility. That power is measured in numbers. They encourage their people to multiply and outnumber the other religions. Hence we see the Islamic and Catholic attitudes to large families and resistance to contraception. They do not care for this world. Their sights are firmly set on the next. This world can be destroyed just as long as the population believes in their brand and choice of deity. They will create war, strife and genocide in order to win over a larger percentage of the population even if it results in everyone's demise.

To tackle the population explosion globally all these issues need addressing. I suggest the United Nations is given emergency powers to make world population control its prime aim.

Safari in Zimbabwe and Botswana

Nothing quite prepared me for me first experience of a safari.

While travelling through Zimbabwe we stopped at a safari lodge for our first real expedition out into the African bush.

It started at 5.30 a.m. which is not usually a good time for me. We had to be out in the bush in time for the dawn when the animals were out about feeding. By the middle of the day it was too hot and they tended to rest in the shade. We huddled on the truck wrapped in blankets against the morning chill and headed off into the dark bumping and careering down the rutted tracks.

By the time the sun was up we were well into the reserve and heading for the action. The first sightings were of a large female giraffe grazing on the top leaves of a thorny acacia tree with new-born baby giraffe, on spindly legs, in tow. She lazily watched us, chewing earnestly, as we drew near and seemed content for us to be close but not too close. She kept a wary eye on our progress. Our guide was experienced and knew just how far to push it.

We were up close and personal with my first 'game' animal in the wild and I was surprised to find myself so absolutely elated. I had seen many giraffes in zoos right up in touching distance and had even fed one by hand but had not been particularly moved. This was entirely different.

I was hooked.

For the next two hours we bumped and skidded around delightedly discovering a whole range of wild animals. Excitedly we sneaked up on eland, antelope, warthogs, gazelle and elephant along with numerous multi-coloured birds of all sizes.

By the time we got back for breakfast I was buzzing.

I had to do another.

By the time we got round to the incredible Victoria Falls I was more than eager. We went and looked at the falls and briefly considered the bunji jump from the bridge before deciding that it was an experience better foregone. All that was in my head was getting out to the reserve in Botswana for a second dose of safari.

Again we set off in the early morning and went hurtling down tracks. The driver appeared to be a maniac who had escaped from Brands Hatch. We clung on for dear life and found ourselves in deep meditation as if our mental powers might keep the truck upright.

Our guide must have had x-ray vision. Every now and then he'd screech to a halt in a cloud of dust and show us some exotic coloured birds ensconced in a tree of deep in a bush, a snake or a small animal crouched in the recesses of a rock. His powers were legendary.

Somehow, despite the periods of rally driving, he managed to find the animals and more amazingly, insinuate us among them without creating panic. We edged forward right into the midst of a group of warthogs rolling about in a muddy pool; he pulled up alongside hyenas, eland, zebra, gazelles and giraffe. It was masterly.

Our driver was not content. He explained to us that no safari was complete without a herd of elephant and he believed he knew where they might be hiding.

We charged back through the bush, hurtling down the narrow tracks at great speed. Suddenly we careered to a skidding halt which nearly ended up as a broadside. There standing right across the trail blocking our path was a great bull elephant. Behind him in the bush we could glimpse and hear the crashing of the rest of the herd. Our bull stood in the path with his big ears flapping as if on guard, which he undoubtedly was, while the herd moved off further in the bush and disappeared into the distance. He looked annoyed and possibly belligerent.

I was mesmerised. I had never been that close to a wild wild-animal.

That elephant looked as if he meant business and might really charge us. I could see our driver was thinking along the same lines as he had his hands on the gear-stick and had slipped it into reverse with his foot poised over the throttle.

We were all motionless. He stared at us, swished his tail and flapped his ears in vexation and looked disgruntled. You could see he was not amused. We sat motionless and refrained from breathing.

I reviewed the numerous anecdotes I had heard regarding bull elephants and unwary safari members and found myself wondering how fast a truck could go in reverse. I also found myself extremely grateful that we had a frustrated racing driver as a guide. Even so it seemed a tall order on such a narrow, rutted, dusty track. I thought the elephant might win and found myself weighing up the possibility that it might even be preferable to have your truck impacted by a mad bull elephant rather than smashed into a tree and overturned. I decided neither was too desirable.

Mr. Elephant, as I respectfully addressed him telepathically, finally made up his mind and turned his back on us to stalk off into the bush after the herd.

Our driver seemed strangely unperturbed and assured us that we were in safe hands; he had been completely in control. He promptly careered off down another track intent on intercepting the herd at a suitable point where we might get a close look at the rest of the group.

I thought this was extremely foolhardy and reckless behaviour, or else the actions of a highly knowledgeable and experienced expert on elephant behaviour and regardless of which it was urged him on to get a move on.

Before long we had overtaken the herd and parked up in a bit of a clearing as they ambled past ripping at branches with their trunks and grazing on vegetation without showing any too much concern for us. Even Mr. Elephant seemed to accept that we were essentially harmless and we were able to soak in our fill of the tiny babies, big mothers and assorted others. What an amazing experience.

It was only a big nature reserve criss-crossed with tracks made by land-rovers and trucks. It was not quite in the same league as being out in the untrammeled wilderness as it had been long ago. It would have been wondrous to have travelled back in time to those days long ago before there were such things as trucks and guns. But it certainly gave you a flavour.

I was breathing the dust. I was back in Africa where my ancestors had lived, back among the wild beasts they would have hunted with their primitive flint weapons. Back where they would have beat off the lions and leopards with the teamwork and intelligence that made us so successful.

This was living.

Second safari of the day in Botswana

Following the blistering success of our first safari in Botswana we were already booked on the second. This promised to be a slightly more sedate affair. It was basically a leisurely afternoon cruise up the Zambezi in a flat bottomed small boat.

It promised to be an extremely pleasant experience and quite a contrast to the morning as the movement of the boat created a pleasant breeze in the unrelenting heat and this cooling effect was augmented by the cold bottle of beer that was placed in my hand. It all made for a pleasant relaxed atmosphere.

The first thing our intrepid captain did was to sidle right up amongst a pod of huge hippopotami whose massive heads were protruding from the water with big eyes peering back at us and little ears twitching. We could easily have reached out to touch them but refrained knowing that might be pushing things a tad too far.

It was a little disturbing as I was well aware of the reputation of hippos. They might look nice and placid but they were dangerous animals. If they had become annoyed or feared for their calves they could have easily overturned our little craft and dumped us in the crocodile infested waters. Our craft was quite small and flimsy. They are extremely defensive of their young and there were a number of little ones among the group. My apprehensions proved groundless and we survived to see more. We were not charged, trampled and drowned by mad hippos and they were a docile delight.

Further up stream we cruised right up to great crocodiles basking on the river bank with huge open mouths cooling themselves in the sun. They looked hot but they weren't getting my beer though.

An extremely large monitor lizard picked its way gingerly across the broad-leafed waterweed, its tongue darting forth as it scented the air in search of prey.

The icing on the cake was when a great herd of elephants came out of the bush and down to the water completely out in the open complete with little babies running in and out of their mother's legs.

The elephants proceeded to have great fun squirting each other and cooling off. Their great ears flapped as they sucked up water and threw their trunks up in the air as they squirted it over their backs. The water sprayed through the air in streams of glistening droplets and splattered over their backs turning the dusty grey to dark black. You could feel the joy of it.

The sun was setting. I had another chilled beer and felt completely sated with life. I could have stayed on safari for ever.

Sadness on safari and Chinese medicine superstition

There is something magical about animals in the wild, untamed, free and dangerous. It sets the blood rushing.

I have sat by water-holes as the animals come in to drink and watched the herds come in and drift back off into the bush. It is a very satisfying sight. I have also got up right up alongside a range of large beasts from the back of a truck and by small boat.

A wild animal is a regal, haughty beast that is nothing like the specimens you see in zoos and circuses. There's a psychological factor at work I'm sure. Not matter how big the cage they are not free to roam and you are separated from them by a cage. They are cooped up and they know it. They are no longer free. For me it is like comparing a fat fluffy pussy-cat with a majestic wild tiger.

I would prefer that my tigers were not made into tame pussy-cats.

We have two lots of friends who regularly go to Africa on safari. They are so hooked by the experience that they do not go anywhere else. For them it is nearly always Kenya and the Masai Mara.

They have gone especially to witness the great migration of the large herds of wildebeest migration on the Serengeti and felt the awe as they crossed the rivers. They've seen prides of lions close up, leopards with their kill in trees, giraffe, rhino, zebra, herds of gnu, eland, dik-dik and most other things. There is a great connection of humans with the type of nature our ancestors grew up with.

On the last occasion one set of our friends went to Kenya they returned with tales of gloom and despair. They felt the wild-life they cherished was being systematically ravaged. Instead of herds of elephants visiting the water-holes they were seeing single forlorn stragglers. Even the small creatures were becoming rare and disappearing at an alarming rate.

Their guides told them that it was the Chinese immigrants. China had been making huge investments in Kenya and large numbers of Chinese had moved in. The guides claimed that these workers had a different attitude to wild life - if it moved you ate it! If you could not eat bits you could harvest it for medicinal use. All over the world tigers, elephants and rhinos were being senselessly slaughtered to satisfy the market for superstitious Chinese medicine.

It is insane madness. Much of the medicine does not even work.

For many Chinese the tiger was thought to give you great power and vitality if it was eaten. Its bones can be crushed and eaten. Tiger penises were supposed to give you great potency.

The rhino horn also was a provider of great potency. I'm not sure what the elephant tusk is meant to do. But I really wouldn't want to have a penis the size of those dimensions anyway!

It seems crazy to me that in this supposed age of science we have a resurgence of superstition based on ignorance and stupidity.

I have nothing against old folk-lore. There have been many elements of good practice that has emanated from some of it. The use of various herbs in the treatment of a range of illnesses has been useful. We have extracted many useful drugs out of these including such things as aspirin from willow bark. However, this good information is mixed in with a lot of fallacious information, some of which, as with tiger bone, is completely loopy and some of which is positively harmful. A number of supposed Chinese remedies have been shown to contain powerful toxins that do a lot more harm than good. Some are so dangerous they can kill.

The ancients were not a font of great wisdom as many would claim. They were largely ignorant, illiterate, uneducated and did not have the benefit of scientific methodology. Their wisdom is flawed and limited. A lot of it is based on quasi-religious nonsense and superstitious stupidity.

Rhino horn is keratin. That is the same substance as is found in hair and nails. It does not have any other useful ingredients and neither does it possess any great magical powers. That is because there are no magical powers. It has no medicinal value and absolutely no effect on male impotence.

The ancients prescribed rhino horn because of its physical attributes. Because it was hard and erect they believed it would miraculously have the same effect on human penises. This is an example of limp thinking. You can have as much effect by biting your own nails. Yet rhinos are presently being hunted to extinction because of this ignorant fallacy. Rhino horn is worth considerably more than gold.

Likewise tigers are big, powerful and fierce but that does not mean that eating them, their bones or penises, will have any greater effect than eating any other meat. You've as much chance of growing spikes on your back from eating hedgehogs or scales and fins from eating fish.

It is manifestly absurd. Yet we are down to the last few thousand wild tigers because of this imbecility.

When will we finally become rational? We are like little children believing in fairy-tales. In the real world you use science to cure you. If you are impotent see a doctor and get a prescription for some drug that will work rather than a quack superstition from an unqualified idiot who is making a nice living out of the trade that is killing our wild life off. Why use ineffective rhino horn when you can have highly effective Viagra at a fraction of the price?

It is obvious to me that all people who practice Chinese medicine, or any other form of superstitious folk-lore, should be made to have a suitable qualification and their products scientifically tested for efficacy and toxicity. If they do not work or are harmful they should be banned. If practitioners use endangered species in their cures they should not only be struck off but imprisoned.

Zambia and flying round the farm

Kathy and Tobes were African. They came over to England in their teens but they always loved Africa. Tobes always wanted to run a farm and after working around in a few dead-end jobs decided to turn his intelligence on to the task of running that farm. He extrapolated back.

It went like this:

To run a farm in Africa I have to be working for the Commonwealth Development Corporation.

To get into the CDC I have to have a first or upper second from one of two universities in Britain.

To get into those universities I have to have seven O Levels in relevant subjects and 3 A Levels in Biology, Chemistry and Maths all with grade As.

So that is what Toby did. He enrolled in the relevant night classes. In year one he took seven O Levels and achieved 7 grade A's. The next year he took his three A Levels and got the necessary grades and went to Bangor University to do the course in agriculture. The fairy tale went on from there.

We went to see them in Zambia where Tobes was running the biggest farm in the southern hemisphere - bigger than anything in Australia.

The CDC was an organisation that was fostering sympathetic development. It cared for the environment and the sympathetic development of Africa for the good of African people.

Tobes believed in that. He developed his huge farm with wheat and coffee plantations and used it to provide work for thousands of

Africans. He provided schools, roads and housing and was instrumental in raising their standard of life.

There was a principle at work. If people worked and could live in harmony with nature, alongside nature, there was a sustainable future.

The downside of the farm was that much of the wilderness was flattened to farm the wheat.

Tobes flew me round the place as it was far too big to ride round. It was amazing and impressive.

If only we could organise the planet so that there was efficient farming, education, and a standard of life for all humans without encroaching too much into the wilderness; so that we did not destroy all the wild life and learned to respect nature; so that we could put aside 50% of the planet for the wild things without encroaching into their world.

We can share this planet. It is not too late to organise that. All we need is the will to do, proper legislation and enforcement.

Kathy and Tobes are an inspiration.

Unfortunately CDC were taken over and the big boys moved in with a view to profitability. The ideals were to be sacrificed on the pyre of profit.

Hull and Urbanisation

When you have lived in an area for a long time you really notice the changes.

I lived in Hull and travelled in every day to Beverley.

Hull is an old city that was once one of Britain's great walled cities. It was a top three port along with Liverpool and London and drew in its prosperity from commerce from all around the world. Hull grew into a thriving, prosperous cosmopolitan city full of ideas, culture and learning. It was affluent and cosmopolitan before the word had even been invented. Unfortunately it later declined as a port and then further on lost its fishing industry. In the Second World War it was the most bombed city in England and a lot of its historic infrastructure was lost though amazingly a fair bit remains. I moved up to Hull from London in 1974.

Beverley was a thriving Market Town twelve miles away from Hull. It prospered and was recently voted the best place to live in England due to its three brilliant schools, great facilities, pleasant surroundings and great ambience.

When I first arrived in Hull I used to get a lift into work with a colleague. We would drive out of the city along a back road through the countryside for twelve miles to Beverley. It was a nice start and end to the day.

That lazy, winding back road has been replaced with a major by-pass. The outskirts of Hull have sprouted new suburbs. The outskirts of Beverley have sprouted new estates. The fields are being built on. It has been an incremental year on year increase in urban sprawl that you adjust to and hardly notice. This last year or so, for example, they have built a big new hospital on a green field site and are putting a big ring-road around Beverley that crosses what once were fields.

The site of scientific important, where I used to take my students to see the voles, is now a housing estate.

The open ditch at the back of my house is now invisible because it has been culvetted in.

There is a creeping urbanisation as wasteland is built on, houses spring up, roads are laid down, trees chopped, ponds filled, ditches filled , hedges uprooted and woods and shrub-land concreted over.

Habitats are being slowly eroded with the steady pace of waves lapping at a cliff. Little by little - year after year it creeps.

The population grows. They need housing and facilities. It is progress.

Then we wake up and wonder why we don't see any hedgehogs anymore. Why is there no frogspawn? What has happened to the butterflies and bees? Where are all the birds?

You don't know what you've got til it's gone!

Los Angeles - a tale of urban sprawl - the air-conditioned nightmare

In1790 there were just 131 people living in the whole of Los Angeles. By 1870 that had risen to 5000 and by 1900 to a mere 100,000. From there on in it was explosive. The population topped 319,000 in 1910 and hit 1,238,000 by 1930. It is currently approaching 4,000,000.

The urban sprawl this has created means that the city incorporated 88 cities and is one of the 20 dirtiest in America.

Presently Los Angeles is fifty miles across. But it wasn't always like that - it started as seven small communities in the midst of a great fertile valley. That fecund valley was farmed extensively and produced orchards of succulent oranges and peaches and fields of squash and melon.

Because the sun was hot, there was good irrigation with rivers from the mountains and the soil was so good the crops were excellent.

Lots of people migrated in to work and experience the great climate. The film industry set up home in Hollywood. Wine from the Napa valley took off in a big way. The surfing was great and the Rock scene burgeoned. There were lots of Mexican immigration and the community just grew and grew and grew.

Gradually the roads and interstates blossomed, housing went up and the city grew and prospered. The urban sprawl spread out and engulfed all the communities around and they were incorporated. The fertile soil was buried under concrete and the whole valley became a huge a huge city with no sign of a natural field or river to be seen.

The sun peered down through the photo-chemical aerosol produced by the endless stream of cars going up the boulevards and interstates, the endless jams, and the natural environment with its entire ecosystem was no more.

The people sit in their jammed traffic on the clogged highways in their air-conditioned cars, or work in their air-conditioned offices, shop in their air-conditioned malls or watch TV in their air-conditioned condos!

We had to take fleeces with us to the restaurants because the air-conditioning was turned up so high it was too cold even though the temperature outside might be roasting.

Henry Miller wrote a novel about it all called - 'The air-conditioned nightmare' in 1939.

He was a prophet of his day.

Chongqing City

Chongqing (Chunking) is the biggest city in the world with a population of 29 million - approximately half the present population of Britain all in one place.

We visited Chongqing after completing the Yangtze River Three Gorges tour. It was bathed in thick smog and a number of the people on the streets were wearing their ubiquitous smog masks. It was smoggy enough to make your eyes water.

Chongqing was a strange mixture of modernity and antiquity. There were incredibly great futurist sky-scrapers and a lot of peasant porters with poles over their shoulders waiting to carry anything moveable. It was incredible how much they could carry in their two baskets.

We did not stay long but were whisked straight out on the highway bound for Xian and the amazing terracotta army.

On the road out we passed through great stretches full of these great towering blocks. Each one was surrounded with a little open space and resembled an extremely large tower-block.

Our Chinese guide, in his usual informative boastful manner when addressing the wonderful progress being made by China with its economic miracle, was boasting to us about the fact that only a few years before all this used to be paddy-fields. Now we had this brilliant new super-highway and all these great new homes for the people.

Each one of these blocks was a whole autonomous town. They contained health facilities, police, shops, schools and everything a person could possibly need. There was no need for anyone to have to go outside.

I knew what it did not contain - it did not contain a tiger.

The great tower blocks in the countryside made my eyes water again.

A cat in the road

I hate cruelty to animals. I know they have the same nervous systems as us, the same biochemistry and feel pain in the same way we do. Once you have got close to an animal you can empathise with them; you can feel the spectrum of emotions they are capable of. Animals are different to us. They have a different psychology. That is undeniable. But there is no one on this planet can persuade me that when someone gaffs a porpoise or dolphin with a great barbed hook that it does not feel the pain. A dolphin has a bigger brain than us. It has language and social interaction. When someone tries to saw a dolphin's neck with a knife that is no different to beheading a man or woman; except it is because, in the case of a dolphin, it is anatomically more difficult and takes longer. That dolphin suffers as much agony and terror as you would.

The tragedy of the environmental destruction, pollution, hunting and poisoning of our wild-life is the distress and pain it is causing to so many animals. There is a thoughtlessness and cruelty to what we are doing.

Back in 1972 I was working in an animal house in East London. It involved caring for thousands of animals and also unfortunately having to kill them.

I figured that I could at least make their lives better while they were alive and dispatch them swiftly and painlessly when the time came.

I loved working with the animals and did my best for them. That was how I justified it.

On the way in to work one morning through the London traffic on my motorbike, dressed in my leather jacket with long hair flowing behind me, I saw a nasty accident. A cat ran out into the road in a desperate bid to get to the other side. It was hit by a car and I saw the back wheel of the car go over its back and head.

I instinctively pulled over to the side and went over to it. The cat was yowling piteously. There was blood coming from its ears and it was trying to drag its useless back legs. I could see that its back was broken and its skull fractured. It was not long for this world but it was in agony.

I quickly made an assessment and came to a conclusion; I smacked its head on the kerb and put it out of its misery.

Then I looked up and there was this bus queue of commuters all staring at me with looks of disgust. What they had seen was some Hell's Angel who had smashed the brains out of a poor kitty.

I do not believe we should let any creature suffer if we can possibly help it. That is why I want our natural environment protected.

New research and new dangers

Back in the 1970s we were teaching about food chains and how pollutants like radio-activity, heavy metals and pesticides built up in food-chains to accumulate in large amounts in those at the top of a food chain. As humans were at the top of most food chains it was particularly relevant to us.

The classic study was carried out on DDT. This pesticide was used extensively back in the 1950s and 1960s. It killed insects and was thought to be harmless to humans and higher animals. They sprayed people and homes with it. Everyone believed it only affected insects and was harmless to mammals and that it diluted down in the environment anyway and would naturally degrade. It was then discovered that DDT had a toxicity in mammals that was linked to cancer. It was found that animals as distant as polar bears and penguins in the Polar Regions had huge levels of DDT in their body and that humans too had accumulated extremely high levels. The levels were so high that it would have been illegal to sell human flesh as meat because the DDT levels were many times above the permitted level.

DDT was later banned because of the link to human health plus the fact that it was indiscriminately killing insects whether they were pests or not. This was having a dramatic impact on other animal populations. The food chain/ web meant that all creatures were interconnected. If you killed off one type it impacted everywhere else in the food chain and caused great over-abundance of the creatures the ones you'd killed off fed on and also caused the death of the predators that fed off those that you'd killed. That spelt trouble.

In the 1960's and 1970s British Nuclear fuels used to dump radioactive waste at sea. Greenpeace investigated by following the boats and discovered they were dumping it in shallow water on a fishing ground.

Is there no common sense? We assume the people being paid huge sums of money to make good decisions are capable of doing their job. All too often they cut corners and take the cheapest, easiest option. Any fool can do that. You expect highly paid individuals to know better.

The barrels of nuclear waste corroded and released their contents. This then entered the food chain and we ate the fish. It is quite probable that a number of people contracted cancer from this and died. There is simply no way of proving it.

It is no wonder the public opinion turned against nuclear power. People lost trust in the people running it. We thought they did not do things responsibly and lied about what they were doing.

The same was true of heavy metals such as lead, cadmium, arsenic and mercury. It was quite common to dump industrial effluent containing these heavy metals into the sea. The powers that be believed the effluent was dispersed through the whole body of the ocean. This is not the case; it built up in mud sediments in high concentrations and proved to be extremely patchy in terms of its dispersal.

The adverse effects of mercury poisoning were first made apparent in Japan at the fishing port of Minamata in the 1930s. First people noticed cats with strange behaviour dancing and collapsing in the streets and then it was people losing coordination, shouting and suffering slurred speech. A local company had been discharging mercury salts into the bay. It had entered the food chain and accumulated in the fish and shell-fish the village lived off. The result was a debilitating nervous disease.

Even today there are high levels of mercury in the environment. In South America it is used in gold mining to extract ore and is widely polluting the Amazon and causing severe nerve debilitating disease in the miners and their compatriots.

In Britain and America pregnant women are advised not to eat tuna or too much fish because of mercury.

In Britain lead was added to paint. It was added to petroleum to make engines run more smoothly and pumped out in car exhausts. It even used to be an ingredient of women's cosmetics! Lead piping was standard and the soldering of water pipes was with molten lead. There was consequently lots of lead in the environment that was showing up in people's bodies.

It was only when studies started to emerge that associated lead poisoning with learning disorders and violent behaviour that action was taken.

I remember teaching lessons on football hooliganism in the 1970s. I had pictures of girls being carried out of football stadia with darts stuck in their skulls, penetrating their brains. There was one individual that had a knife jammed into her skull. It was common for groups of youths to go to matches, where the terraces were packed, and throw sharpened coins, darts and throwing knives into the air to come down on people's heads. There was another practice of going to matches with razor sharp Stanley knives and slicing people. Studies made of the instigators showed abnormally high levels of lead in their blood.

The evidence mounted and lead poisoning was found to be involved with violence and disruption of learning. Lead was outlawed from paint, water-pipes, solder and petrol. Since then the level of violent crime has come down year upon year. Many people make the association.

Even small levels of toxins, radio-active isotopes and pesticides can build up in food chains to poison us through our diet, or they can be absorbed from high levels in our direct environment, such as breathing in traffic fumes in inner cities. Fortunately this is now all monitored a lot better, legislated a lot better and our health has improved as a result.

This does not mean we are safe from pollutants. Unfortunately other countries are not so responsible and still dump stuff into the air, fresh water, landfill and sea. Those contaminants end up in our bodies. This is why we need world-wide legislation and enforcement. Pollution does not respect national boundaries.

There are many new chemicals that we do not yet understand the effects of on our food webs or physiology. A good example is the new stories emerging about the effects of diesel particles. They enter and damage lungs and have been implicated in heart attacks and strokes.

We need more research and better legislation and enforcement to protect us and the life we share this planet with.

Nuclear disasters

My daughter's father-in-law used to work in the nuclear industry. He claims to have a solution to both the energy problem and safe disposal of low level nuclear waste.

He claims that it would be possible to vitrify the low level waste into tablets that could be placed in the emersion tanks of every home. The decay would heat the water at no cost and the water and metal of the tank would more than adequately completely shield against any radiation. We are talking of alpha particles here which cannot penetrate a single sheet of paper. The water and metal of a water tank would more than adequately shield us from the radiation.

It will never happen. The nuclear industry has massive problems convincing the public that it is safe. That is not surprising as they have demonstrated time and time again that they cannot be trusted.

They have dumped radio-active waste at sea in the most stupid of places. My classes of high school students came up with better places to dump it. Why are we paying huge salaries to people who are incompetent and deceitful? They dumped barrels of nuclear waste in shallow water on a fishing ground? Are they nuts?

They build nuclear plants in the most stupid places. Why would anyone build a nuclear plant on an earthquake fault line as in California or in an area subject to earthquakes and tsunamis as in Japan?

Why would anyone cover up nuclear disasters and continue to sell contaminated milk that they know will cause cancer and death, to school-children? This is what happened in the 1950s when Windscale, our first nuclear reactor, suffered a meltdown. This was in the early days of the nuclear industry when nuclear was being heralded as a safe and cheap way of producing energy. The government of the day thought it best not to scare people and put them off the nuclear adventure. So they hushed it up and sold contaminated milk. Many of us thought that the only reason they wanted nuclear power, which was more expensive than other forms of production, was in order to get fissionable material for the construction of nuclear weapons. This was, of course, hotly denied. I still believe that was the reason.

Why would anyone play about testing the limits of safety in a nuclear plant? Which seems to be what happened at both Three Mile Island and Chernobyl disasters.

These seem like the errors a school-child might make. It doesn't make for a great amount of trust in the industry does it? - Too much pollution, too many risks, too many poor decisions and too much harm to the environment.

When will we learn?

The Spain field-trip

I am an entomologist which is why I went on a botany field-trip to Alicante in Spain with my mates Pete Smith, Pete Auber and Pete Phelby who were all also entomologists just like me.

It was Easter 1971 and the Botany department had organised a field-trip. Unfortunately a number of people dropped out and it wasn't financially viable any longer. They decided to open it up to Biologists. As it was just prior to finals and most students were diligently planning to utilise the time doing some highly necessary revision they did not get a lot of takers. Thus it fell on our shoulders to save the day. By volunteering, and sacrificing our revision time, we enabled those Botanists to get their field-trip. I do not think we ever got the recognition for that decision.

As there was no supervisory entomologist we were left to our own devices. We were expected to organise our own educational experience. On arrival we discovered a huge beetle and a glow-worm in the drive of the chalet. It augured well.

The Botanists headed off each day weighed down with transects piles of books and equipment. We headed off in the other direction with some collecting jars and stopped off at the shops to stock up with vino, bread and cheese.

The place was swarming with life. There were big black scorpions under the rocks, snakes swimming along the gulleys, lizards galore and a huge toad. We collected the scorpions. Pete chased a very big snake in a field and caught it just before it disappeared into a dry stone wall. He grabbed its tail and pulled and got a shock when the snakes head shot out of the wall at him. It had snaked back on itself!

We took to sitting in the gulley drinking the wine and having a laugh while the wild life came to us. It was so alive with insects you did not have to look for them - they looked for you! We sat there and played with them and made a token collection to take back. We even recorded the specimens we found - at least Pete Auber did. He was very diligent. It was an entomologist's paradise. We loved it. I collected a couple of egg clusters that seemed to be all over the place. I was sitting at college a few weeks later when someone noticed these insects crawling over me. The egg batches were preying mantids and I had a dozen baby mantids emerging to infest me. Great fun!

I believe Pete Auber even wrote it up when we got back! He had a species list and all sorts. All I had was a hang-over!

Fairly recently I went back to Alicanti. The place had been built up to the point where I could not recognise it. The fields and wild places had gone. There were no glow-worms, beetles or other insects around. The snakes and scorpions were gone. There were not even any gulleys to study in.

It had gone from a feast to a famine in thirty years.

Portugal and the chameleons

In 1973 our friends Dan and Carol had a VW minibus and we all decided to go off to Portugal in the van. As our son Dylan was only three months old it was a little bit of an undertaking but it did not perturb us all that much. We were used to camping. All we were concerned about was the effect of the heat on a three month old baby. We were reassured by the doctor that he would cope better than us. His surface to volume ratio was greatly in his favour.

We burned our way through France and Spain, dropping off at the Prado Art Gallery to take in the Hieronymus Bosch's, before arriving in Portugal.

It was like stepping back in time. We were amazed to see people going along on little asses and horses and carts vying with new Mercedes on the roads. The Algarve was largely untouched and there were quaint fishing villages with people still in old-fashioned costumes.

We got a basket load of sardines from one of the small boats. It had come in with a hold full to brimming with sardines. A fisherman was standing up to his chest in fish. They threw baskets down to him and he dipped them in and flung them back up full of fish. There was no mechanisation at work here and there was no over-fishing of sardines as far as I could tell. Sardines were plentiful.

We negotiated for a basket of fish and he gave us one for free. They had fish enough to burn. We went back and fed the entire camp-site.

It was boiling hot where we were but the local old ladies all had great heavy voluminous dresses, usually in black as there was always someone who had died in the family, which must have been unbearable in the heat. They chastised us roundly for not covering Dylan up. They were shocked to see us keeping him naked in his Moses basket. Yet the temperature was well into the nineties.

To cool off we went into the shade of the pines near the camp-site. That was when we discovered they were infested with chameleons. The unusual lizards gripped the branches and sat motionless waiting for insects to come near so that they could grab them with their whip-like sticky tongues. They walked along the branches in slow-motion looking like they were doing robotic dance movements on mogadon.

We put them on different coloured backgrounds to watch how quickly they changed colour. They were amazing.

I wonder if there are still any of them about? The Algarve is different now. It is all built up and has become a major tourist attraction. I suspect the sleepy fishing villages and the chameleons are just memories.

Australian Wonderland

In 2013 I finally got to visit with Pete and Trudy in Australia. We got into Newcastle, after being picked up in Sydney and stopping on the way back to sample some bubbly and survey the pelican's, and the temperature soared. In our car the thermometer was registering 50 degrees. It was a record!

Our friends in England thought we were causing calamities. We'd flown into Tasmania to the sweet smell of bush-fires, arrived in Newcastle to record temperatures that went on to hurricanes, record flooding and further bush-fires. We didn't cause it - honest!

Pete and Trudy's terrace in the garden was the start of the wonderland. Australia is still relatively unspoiled. The population is small and concentrated in the five or six big cities leaving a lot of untouched wilderness. Apart from the road-kill attrition, the logging and land stripped for farming and urban development there is a lot of space for wild life. Taking a glass of wine on the terrace and looking over the garden allows you to begin to commune with nature. As we talked to our dear friends the Cockatoos squawked and performed in the trees, turning upside down, displaying and destructively ripping the trees up. In the flowering trees around the terrace the rainbow lorikeets were drinking themselves into a stupor on the nectar and cavorting in the branches like mobile rainbows. There were large golden orb spiders in their webs and frogs croaking in the pond. We were surrounded with the sweet orchestra of nature.

Later we took the dogs for a walk and there was a great big water-dragon in the grass. It promptly got up on its hind-legs and ran.

We were to see lots more parrots and lizards as we went round including the wonderful crimson rosella and the crazy long-billed corellas who seemed to love falling over and playing with each other. The Black cockatoos put on the most amazing displays with their red plumage showing.

Our first trip out was to the Tamworth Country Festival where all the denizens of the outback seemed to congregate for a week of Australian Country music which is like nothing else on Earth. On the way there we stopped off at Moghen and Bente's and their incredible house they'd built in the hills in the middle of nowhere. Bente took in injured animals and was nursing a small Joey wallaby whose mother had been killed in a motor accident. She was carrying it around in a sling and feeding it milk from bottles. She got the young traumatised, injured youngsters fit and healthy and released them back into the wild where they seemed to get accepted back into the local community of wallabies without too much trouble. Bente had one fully grown male that she'd successfully released the year before. He still came when she whistled and took a bottle of milk. It was wonderful to see.

On the way back from the festival Trudy spotted an echidna scuttling along at the side of the road. We stopped and Pete and I got thick gardening gloves on and picked it up to get a good look. It was incredible to hold it and see its powerful limbs and little pointed snout. It was like a creature from times gone past.

As we drove on, having put that echidna somewhere a bit safer, away from the highway, Pete noticed that his foot was feeling soggy and sticky in his sandal. We stopped and he discovered his sandal was swimming with blood. There appeared to be a little nick on his toe that wouldn't stop bleeding. At first we thought he's cut it on something when we were looking at the echidna but when the wound wouldn't stop bleeding we twigged that it had been a leech that had caused it. It had latched on painlessly and injected an anti-coagulant which was why the small puncture refused to clot. We checked the car and there in the well, under the mat, was this ginormous leech as bloated as a blimp with Pete's blood.

A bit of blood is a small price to pay for such wonders. We sent it back into the river in a gentle loop through the air. Everything has its place in the beautiful woven web of life.

More Australian wonders

The wonders in Australia never ended. When we met up with Pete and Trudy to camp our way back to Newcastle along the amazing coast it was one astounding thing after another. We camped in the bush and a kookaburra was actually tame enough to take meat out of your hand, big goannas ran up trees, a wallaby with baby sticking out of her pouch sat near our tent in the undergrowth, the sea was alive with rainbow fish and coral, a couple of huge goanna stalked past through the undergrowth, bell birds sang in the tree-tops, cockatoos flew overhead in pairs, and water-dragons lay in the sun.

What more could you want.

At night the possums came round and scavenged for food, taking marsh mallows out of your hand. A bandicoot kept popping into sight and scuttling about through the kitchen area. At one time we had three possums and the bandicoot all around us. It was heaven. Trudy even got to stroke one of the possums.

We stayed with Pete and Trudy's friends on their huge estate. We had bats flying round our room at night, waded in the lake pulling out the water lilies that were choking it up, (later being informed that there were highly poisonous water-snakes to be found in among the lilies) looking at the eagles, hunting for wombat who pounded off through the trees before we could get a good sight of one. I got to see them though.

All that and there wasn't a redback spider or brown snake to be seen.

We headed off for the incredible Blue Mountains and marveled at the stupefying panorama of nature. The sun set on the seven sisters and it was idyllic. We hiked down into the basin and found orange crayfish and an eel in the stream.

I had taken quite a fancy to bark and spent time photographing the beautiful coloured bark with its patterns. The eucalyptus trees and gum trees, the paper bark and dozens more. There were trees with reds, yellows and greens, bark with squiggly lines eaten out by larvae.

The house we staying in had a crimson rosella in the garden. There were cockatoos, lorikeets and birds of paradise.

If it could only stay that way forever! If only the population stayed that size, the trees weren't sold for mush and the land wasn't ripped to pieces.

I hope to hell it stays as pristine!

The start of Greenpeace

Greenpeace was based in Goodwin Street. I love that!

The first thing I did when I became Head of Biology was to order a whole load of posters and teaching aids from Greenpeace. I felt it was the best use of education money I could find.

I love the story of Greenpeace and how it came into existence. It came right out of that old sixties idealism. We all knew that we can change the world and we did. Unfortunately we did not change it as much as we wanted. The greedy, selfish culture of growth at all costs is still churning its way through the world relentlessly gobbling up everything in its path. The small voice of intelligence and responsibility crying out for a sustainable future is drowned out in the din.

In the face of that madness Greenpeace was an inspiration to us all. It showed that even one man fueled with passion and determination, courage and fearlessness, could take on and beat the Goliath of the State.

Greenpeace came out of the 'Don't Make a Wave' committee which was a loose group of people opposed to the exploding of nuclear weapons underground on a small island in Alaska. Then the government of the France in all its glorious wisdom was intent on carrying out nuclear explosions in the atmosphere in the South Pacific at Moruroa Atoll in French Polynesia. Despite all the protests concerning world-wide radiation fall-out pollution they bullishly made their plans and went ahead. In the early 1970s the nascent Greenpeace chartered a boat which they named 'Greenpeace' and amid huge publicity sailed off with the stated aim of getting as close to the bomb as they could. David McTaggart sailed a small 12.5 metre ketch right up to the test site and around the bomb and held up the operation until he was rammed and sunk. McTaggart was arrested and beaten so severely he lost the sight in one eye. The outcry was immense.

The next year he was back just as determined and the French were forced, through huge public outcry, to halt their atmospheric testing. McTaggart's bravery had defeated the might of a major world power. Anything was possible. No nation was free to commit environmental crimes with impunity. Someone was watching, monitoring and reporting their actions and relaying it around the world. Those people were organisation like Greenpeace and Friends of the Earth.

Greenpeace then took off and became a major force in focusing attention on the wrongs that governments were committing against the environment. They took up campaigns against the wholesale harpooning of whales. People did not know that these glorious intelligent creatures were being shot with great harpoons that exploded in their bodies and sent out huge barbs into its flesh to secure the harpoon while the whale slowly died from its internal injuries. They did not know that whales took up to half an hour to die in agony. They did now.

Whaling was banned. The countries participating were shamed by world opinion and outrage at their inhumanity. Only Japan still defies the ban and acts like barbarians.

Greenpeace then turned their attention to the clubbing of baby seals on the artic ice, the dumping of nuclear waste at sea, effluent from factories, and atmospheric pollution from coal-fired power stations that was causing Acid Rain. Wherever they went they used peaceful 'Non-violent Direct Action' to put themselves in the line of fire. They got themselves between the whale and the harpoon, the barrel and the sea, the club and the seal, and bore witness to the crimes being committed in the name of governments of all persuasions. They were no respecters of national boundaries and pursued campaigns behind the Iron Curtain and in China. They were arrested and imprisoned but that proved no deterrent. They flooded these clandestine grubby operations with the bright light of publicity. The French Government actually deployed frogmen to put limpet mines on the Greenpeace ship 'The Rainbow Warrior' and sunk it with loss of life. They were found out and had to shame-facedly pay compensation. Where-ever an environmental crime was being committed Greenpeace would pop up and tell the world about it. They were masters of publicity. Gradually they put a stop to the bad practice and forced governments and companies to clean up their act.

Those people are my heroes.

The only question I would ask is why? Why should we need Greenpeace at all? If governments behaved responsibly in the first place and did not sanction things being done on the cheap Greenpeace would not be necessary.

I look forward to a world where we won't need champions such as Greenpeace and Friends of the Earth. Let us hope that day comes very soon.

Until then I am proud that we have people who are prepared to put their own lives on the line to protect our environment and the plants and animals that inhabit this jewel of a planet.

We need our real heroes seeing as how Superman is really only a comic strip.

Mass migrations

There are bodies in the water and there are going to be a lot more.

There are gunboats patrolling seas and internment camps and this is just the start.

As the population pressure starts to really bite and people get desperate they will try to escape. It is a biological response to overcrowding. This is the lemming factor, the locust swarm, the reason our ancestors left Africa. When there is too high a density then the psychological response is to move.

When half the world has nothing, and that includes their future, and the other half seem to have everything they could possibly desire then there is an envy that eats into the soul. It drives people to take desperate measures.

Half the world despises the extravagance, waste and care-free existence lived by the other half. They want it too yet they are denied. If they could only get there they could have it. They would do anything to get there.

When the half that have nothing constantly see the lives of the ones that have it all flaunted in their face through the wondrous power of technology, through advertising, through TV and internet, it creates jealousy.

Those desperate people who have nothing to lose either pick up a weapon and join an extreme fascist religious sect, that decries the other half as blaspheming scum and desire to destroy them, or they take every risk to get to the other side, join them and try their best to get their share of the action.

There are bodies falling out of the sky as they freeze crouched in the wheel compartments of high altitude planes. There are suffocated bodies pulled out of containers and lorries. There are piles of bleached bones in the desert.

Every day ships, boats and rafts are intercepted, crammed to the last inch with people with haunted eyes, and they are turned back only to reappear the day after, and the day after that, until they either sink or make it through. Bodies are pulled out of stinking holds. Bloated bodies are floating face down and bobbing up and down with the waves.

Every one of those bodies is an indictment of an unjust world system.

All the time ruthless exploiters are extorting huge sums of money with promises of safe passage and jobs. They lead people across deserts, on to packed boats and into containers. They lead people up the garden path and take their money. They lead people into forced prostitution and slavery with visions of a paradise that is as unreal as paradise.

As the effects of global warming begin to bite it is going to get dramatically worse. As the rains fail, as the floods come, as the seas encroach, as the deserts grow, as the crops fail the people will become more desperate. As the war comes and the battle for resources hots up then the people will try to escape. Anything is better than the hell they find themselves in.

When you have nothing you have nothing to lose. When you don't care if you live or die death is not obstacle.

So what do we do?

Do we step up the interceptions and put more money into the process of preventing them getting in? Do we build more internment camps to hold them? Do we repatriate more people back to the hell they came from and wash our hands of it? Do we hand out aid to the starving people living in those hell-holes in the hopes that they might stay where they are and not bother us?

Or do we try to do something about the root cause of the problem?

I say we try to address the problem!

We take measures to stop the global warming that will exacerbate the problem.

We make it a priority to reduce population density so that there are not all these desperate people with no work and no future.

We create a fairer system where there is not such inequality that creates the hatred, envy and extremism.

I did not say that this is going to be easy. Our whole system needs changing. The system that is based on greed, selfishness, expansion and acquisition of huge wealth by a few is flawed. It is creating the problem. It creates mass poverty in order to exploit it for cheap labour to maximise profit. We need to use our intelligence to change it and we need to change it globally.

We either do that or we suffer the consequences.

The crazy downward spiral into a fight for space, food, dwindling natural resources and water has just begun.

The way I see it is that we have two choices: we either pull together and begin to tackle the global problem we have created or we pull apart, try putting the stopper in the bottle, keep the lid on the pressure cooker and wait for it to blow up in our faces.

Australia - still going

The Australian aborigines had the right idea. Like the American Indians and South American Indians they lived a sustainable life-style in harmony with the planet. They were able to do this because they had relatively small numbers of people. When that life-style was taken away from them by the arrival of the avaricious white culture they sank into alcohol and despair. Their depression has lasted centuries but there are many lessons we can take from their culture. It is time they came out of the shadows and started leading.

The first lesson is to limit your numbers.

The second is to respect the land and all that lives in it.

The third lesson is to care for each other.

Life has evolved over inconceivable millions of years. It has adapted to its environment.

One of the marvels that Pete and Trudy showed me is the remarkable banksias tree seeds and the paper bark tree.

Regularly lighting starts bush-fires. They blaze uncontrollably through the dry undergrowth fuelled by the oils from the gum trees. They are a natural occurrence and not unsurprisingly life has adapted to it.

The paper bark tree has a thick insulating layer of bark that protects it against the great heat of a bush fire.

The banksias are even more incredible. They rely on bush-fires to propagate their seeds. The seeds are protected within insulated pods. These only open after they have been exposed to the great heat of a forest fire. Then they open and the seeds are ejected. In the aftermath of a forest fire the ground has been cleared. The first to germinate has the advantage. Evolution has operated to give the banksias that advantage.

Life is wonderful and adaptable - with or without us.

Uneducated education

Pete and I both found ourselves being forced through an education system that did not do what it said on the tin. It did not educate.

To us education was a wondrous thing. It opened the mind to all possibilities and gloried in the revealed wonders. It unleashed creativity in an explosion of fun. It unlocked potential and sent it soaring. It shone a search-light into the universe and revealed the majesty of what was out there.

Education was ecstasy.

Except ours wasn't. Our education was boring, reductionary, knowledge-laden, mind-numbing, tedious, social controlling, clap-trap. It was terrible.

We both did Biology. We were both nature lovers who had grown up in the ditches of the English countryside. We loved animals, plants and the natural world. That was the reason we had become biologists. What we got lumbered with was facts that reduced things down to less than what they were. Instead of wonder, awe and mind expansion we got a series of facts to learn that in no way revealed the incredible majesty of what we were studying.

We wanted more.

We rebelled.

Pete went off to set up his own company - Smithworks - and his own sets of scientific exploratory sets for kids - Wild Science. He'd given up on the system, decided it was crap and set about doing his own thing. It was wonderful and revolutionary.

Science should be exploration, investigation and discovery. It should leave people reeling with the marvels of nature. It should induce a greater respect and love for animals, plants and nature. If it doesn't do that it has failed no matter how many facts you have crammed your head with.

I went on a different, probably less risky journey, and set about trying to change the system from the inside. I altered the biology curriculum I taught to deal with wonder. I played with the subject to divulge that wonder I had experienced. I tried to turn students on to a love of nature. I tried to teach and relate as an ordinary human being and not a highfalutin authority figure. Ironically it led me to become a Headteacher and an attempt to get the whole school to deal with wonder. It was highly successful.

I believe in education. I believe it is the only way forward.

I believe that we have to educate people to understand the beauties of the world, the delicate nature of the ecosystem, the robustness of nature and our place in it.

To a biologist it is simple. We are not above the animals. We are an animal. No more and no less.

I think we would understand this fact a lot better if we were not the only species of human left on this planet. Oh how we miss the Neanderthal. If there were a number of different species of intelligent humans then perhaps we would not believe we were unique and be so arrogant as to place ourselves in a different category to everything else. Perhaps we wouldn't have the arrogant notion that we were placed in charge and everything was merely put her for us to use and abuse; that it was worthless and without a soul. Perhaps we would not have the crazy idea that we were the pinnacle of creation. Perhaps we wouldn't have created the mumbo-jumbo of religion and superstition that comes up with rubbish such as 'you are the chosen people' and 'the world is given to you to do with as you please'.

We are not the pinnacle of creation. We are probably not even the most intelligent organism on this planet. That might conceivably be a dolphin. The world was not given to us. We evolved on it along with all the other forms of life. We are nothing special. We will come and we will go as every other form of life has done and will do. The only difference we have is that we have evolved greater intelligence than most and have the binocular vision and opposable thumb that has enabled us to develop technology and have a lot more control over what happens to us. Without those two features that have evolved from our brachiating past as monkeys and apes we would not have been able to express our intelligence in developing tools.

Every cell of every creature on this planet has evolved for exactly the same length of time. No organism is more evolved than another. We are all just filling a niche. Some of us are more complex than others but that does not make us better. We are no greater than the bacteria growing under the rim of our toilets.

We are part of this incredible web of life on this planet. We are all profoundly interconnected with each other, the climate, geology and seasons. The system is buffered and will survive whatever we do (short of a major catastrophic event that destroys the planet or sends us into a runaway greenhouse effect as with Venus). We could knock it back to bacterial slime and it will evolve back up again. But I rather like this tangled web of life we have at present. I am partial to the one we have at the moment and would like to hang on to it for a lot longer. I have hopes for mankind. I think we can transcend the lamentable state we are in and build something sustainable that is beautiful. We are better than what we have been. I like to feel that our best moments are still ahead.

That is why I am writing this book.

There are thousands and millions of people just like me who believe we can do it.

What we need is good education. We have to make the children understand that they need to respect life and love nature, that we cannot go on destroying it with impunity and that we can live sustainably.

We have to educate them to use their vast resources of brain power to solve the problems of the world and not just to accrue more wealth for themselves.

That is good education. That is the kind of education Pete and I would be proud of.

South Africa and the whale

Kathy and Toby were living in South Africa and invited us out. I don't need too much encouragement to go to Africa. I love it.

After spending time in Cape Town, climbing up Table Mountain, walking the beautiful beaches in the warm sun, peering at the townships, watching the baboons at the Cape of Good hope, visiting the colony of Humboldt penguins that inhabited a beach further out, and heading across to Robben Island to see where they incarcerated the magnificent Nelson Mandela, we headed out to a game reserve.

Kathy and Tobes had organised a week in a lovely isolated house on the coast in a nature reserve.

We had an adventure on our very first day. Having driven down from Cape Town we arrived in the late afternoon and foolishly wanted to stretch our legs and go for a bit of a walk, partly to see the place and partly out of sheer exuberance.

We got our maps out and picked out a nice little loop of about eight miles. It involved walking along the rocky shore which zigzagged about and went up and down a lot on the jagged cliffs. Then at the end we would go back on a nice trail that led directly back. It was a silly idea really. It was too late and the walk was too long for the time we had. We did not take any proper gear with us, or much food or water. The day was hot and there was a delightful sea breeze.

We set off and gamboled up and down the cliffs, taking in the incredible scenery and full of the joys of being out there free and easy. Because the trail was so windy and up and down it took much longer than we had envisaged. At times we were walking along narrow cliff paths with perilous drops to rocks below and had to take great care. But we were so happy to be there. It was so exhilarating to be under an African sun in such a wondrous place.

We finally reached our destination and realised that it was late. The sun was already going down and in Africa the sun goes down like a lead balloon. One minute it is light and the next it is pitch black.

We looked around for the trail back to the house but it was nowhere to be found. We hunted and hunted in ever increasing circles but no sign of the nice straight trail could be found. The sun set and darkness came.

We debated staying where we were until morning light but we had no clothing and it was already cold. To keep warm we had to move. So we decided to head back. As we could not find the trail and did not fancy trekking into the bush and getting hopelessly lost we decided to go back along the beach trail. It had taken us three hours in the light. It was up on the cliffs with perilous drops. It was dark. You could not see your footing or where the trail was.

Fortunately there was a full moon and it shed a lot of light on proceedings. We picked our way back along the trail, listening out for wild animals and hunting for the wooden logs that had been put in place on the steep bits. We negotiated the cliffs without losing a single one of us and finally made it back to the house long after midnight.

There's nothing like a bit of adventure to get things rolling. It was the start of a magic week.

The place was idyllic. The rollers crashed on the beach and rocks. The sun shone down and bathed us with its warmth.

The wild birds came to our door and sang in the bushes around the house. We climbed the sand-dunes, watched the ostriches and herds of eland and walked along the rocky shores with its hot white sands. We walked close to the zebra, watched the water fowl on the inlet and relaxed to the incredible sunsets that were specially organised just for our benefit.

We came across the skeleton of a huge whale that had been washed up on the beach and played with the parts of the skeleton in awe at its immensity.

The whale symbolises for me, and many others, the many crimes that mankind has committed against nature and the cruelty we so thoughtlessly exhibit. For centuries we have hunted this intelligent and gentle creature and killed it in the most horrendous manner. For all its size and strength, for all its social nature, language and sense of play, for all its ability to survive in the harsh environment of the ocean, it was no match for the technology and viciousness of people. We have slaughtered them and brought them to the edge of extinction.

That whale on that beach was probably not killed by people. It probably died a natural death and was washed up on that beach and picked clean by the scavengers. I hope it had a long and satisfying life, had many progeny and was not terrified by any interaction with my species.

I wish it well.

India a place like no other

We arrived in India to take in the delights of the golden triangle. Despite everything we'd seen we were quite unprepared for the reality.

We knew India had a big population, about 1.2 Billion and rising, but we did not expect them all to be there to greet us. As soon as we got out of the airport we were in the throng of people. The roads were an unbelievable mass of traffic that wove in and out of each other seemingly without any respect for rules or simple laws such as keeping to any particular side. There were camels, buffalo carts, tuk-tuks, cars, trucks (all gaily decorated with carnival decoration, tinsel and swastikas), hand-carts, bikes and people all weaving around and somehow avoiding the numerous cows that placidly lay down or casually chewed amid the chaos.

We started in Delhi and were amazed to find streets lined with ramshackle habitation. Families had piled up bricks to form two walls jutting out from a building, placed sheets of corrugated iron over the top and draped material over the front. In the morning these make-shift curtains would part and a whole family would emerge all immaculately attired. The children would be in perfect clean and ironed school uniform. It was simply staggering. We felt hot and bothered, sweaty and disheveled and we had air-conditioning and a hotel room to go back to with fresh clothes and a shower. The heat was intense, the dirt and squalor all around, there was no electricity or water, apart from a street pump shared by the street, and yet they managed to perform miracles. And education was important. It was the magic key to raise you out of poverty.

Everywhere was piles of rubbish with pigs sifting through and hens pecking. The construction was all with bamboo scaffolding. The Tuk-tuk drivers slept on the seats in their cars. Everywhere was entrepreneurial spirit and ingenuity as all needs were catered for without resources or proper equipment. You could get your machines repaired, patched up, welded, your punctures repaired on the spot, your utensils and equipment serviced. Nowhere in the world is the over-population crisis emphasised more visibly. Nowhere is the pollution more visible.

After visiting the great mosque and absolutely stunning red fort with its intricate sculptured walls, windows and doors with multicoloured inlay, we headed out for Agra and the incredible Taj Mahal.

The site was stunning and I was immediately accosted by a troupe of monkeys who sat on your arms, shoulders and head and ate food from your hands. I adore the kinship with monkeys. I seem to connect with them in some primitive manner. Their touch is exhilarating. I felt the same when we were in Peru and visited a carpet shop in which the owner had a little capuchin monkey as a pet. It was exceptionally take and enjoyed jumping on to you and clinging. It gave me a thrill as well.

Liz dragged me away from the monkeys to look at the beautiful architecture. It was truly breath-taking. But yet again I was taken by the horned antelope in the grounds and an attendant had to shoo me away. He explained they were wild and dangerous and prone to attack with their vicious horns. People had been gored and killed. I was just glad there were wild things left in India. I couldn't believe there was room.

Outside the Taj there was a snake-charmer with a cobra. Liz walked a bit close and it went for her. Fortunately the charmer was alert and astutely grabbed it before it bit. I had heard there were still captive bears that were made to dance and wanted to avoid that cruel misuse of animals.

The Agra fort was almost as amazing as the Taj Mahal and the Red Fort had been.

We headed off through the country-side with its waterways, irrigation and bright green field. This was still peasant farming for the main part with water-buffalo providing the power. They wallowed in their water-holes.

Next it was Jaipur and the incredible Amber Fort, the pink city with the Palace of Sighs and then out to Gwailior Fort with its blue glazed tile insets. We visited a great sandstone gorge with huge Buddhas carved into its walls similar to those of Bamiyan in Afghanistan that were so senselessly destroyed by the Taliban. Here too the Islamic extremists had hacked the faces off the carved Buddhas and they had had to be restored. No faces could be depicted in Islam. That was considered blasphemous and they were intolerant of anybody else's faith or views.

India was an amazing generator of energy and vibrancy. I was struck by its grandeur and its shabbiness. I was also struck by its incredible inequality.

We visited a Maharajas Palace. There was room after room of moldering treasures. Each room was lavishly decorated in a particular style. One room was full of French Impressionist art that actually had mildew growing on them. Another was all ivory and gold. It went on and on. The cost of putting together these priceless collections was simply staggering. Yet outside those grounds there was starvation and disease as a huge population struggled for the basics with which to survive. It epitomised what was wrong with the world. One family could live in such extravagant wealth that their every whim was catered for while outside their door people starved to death.

There is no policy to restrict the population growth. It is all ad hoc. It was full to overflowing yet there did not seem any mechanism short of an epidemic that would solve the problem.

Someone has to come up with something quite soon or there will be standing room only and they will have proved Malthus right.

Australia and Cairns

After our adventures with Pete and Trudy and our Koala on Stradbrooke Island with the distant relatives, now not so distant, we headed off to Cairns for a stay in a room at the side of a lake.

In the centre of Cairns was a tree full of fruit bats and nesting ibis. We'd seen the incredible ibis wandering around in Sydney with their great long black beaks. People in Australia are so blasé about the incredible creatures they are surrounded with that they take it all for granted. I suppose we all do. I take for granted the pheasants and gold finches that come in to my garden. The people of Sydney, Brisbane and Cairns do not find it remarkable when great flying foxes sail across their skyline at dusk or large ibis peck about around them and sit up in the palm trees.

I find it remarkable though. It is part of the rich tapestry of wonders that make up this planet.

In Cairns we got a sky-lift to take us up over the canopy of the rainforest. We watched the rain and mist drift in among the trees, the black cockatoos flying over and the other parrots flitting between trees.

We walked along the empty beaches with their white sand, coconut trees, weird shaped driftwood logs with intricate patterns of bark and wood, and looked out at the sea with its warnings about sea-water crocs and box jellyfish. At least there were no warnings about sharks. The crocs probably ate those.

We went out to Green Island to see the barrier reef and stared at the array of multicoloured fish through the bottom of a glass-bottomed boat, wishing we'd brought snorkeling gear and had longer.

At the cafe we were surrounded with large birds that turned out to be buff-banded rail. They perched on the rails and pecked around the floor and were magnificent.

We walked around the island and took in the brilliance of the scenery. The reef was all around us and the colours were incredible and contrasted with the white of the sand, set off by the great skeletons of dead trees on the beach.

That reef is one of the world's most incredible structures. It is living coral that provides habitats for thousands of special of fish and other marine life. We saw huge turtles gliding through the water, great arrays of anemones, giant clams and sponges. It is a world heritage site. Yet it is under great threat from the warming of the oceans and the acidity of the water. Its days could be numbered; already great swathes of the reef have died.

Our final adventure was to head up into the wilds of the rainforest at Daintree. The plants were huge and so were the spiders that hung in their webs. The golden orbs were the same as we had seen in Louisiana but here they were bigger. Being an arachnophobe I did not go too near to check them out but I could see that they were beautiful in their own big way.

Walking through the rainforest in the humid air and the smell of rotting vegetation is in the all pervasive. I desperately wanted to see a cassowary but they were extremely rare and it seemed unlikely. I'd read a lot about them. They were huge flightless multicoloured birds that resembled psychedelic ostriches. They wandered through the jungles eating fruit whole and digesting the kernels.

We had given up hope when on the way out a family of cassowaries walked out into the road in front of the car. It consisted of a male, female and two offspring. They walked right past us.

It made my year.

On the way back we took a trip up the river to get a close up look at the salt-water crocodiles that were basking on the banks, see the tree frogs, snakes and kingfishers. Our guide pointed out a huge croc who was king of the river. He had once spotted him paddling down the river with a large cow between his jaws.

Our journey through the Australian wonderland was complete.

As Australia starts to find its feet, its economy takes off, partially funded by China, courtesy of extensive strip mining and logging, its population increases, I wonder just how long it will be before it too is denuded and broken?

The present government there seems intent on selling it off to the highest bidder without a thought to the impact and cost.

Road kill yesterday

Yesterday I drove into Hull. It was twenty miles away. The first part is a six mile journey down a windy back lane with hedgerows. Fifteen miles out of the twenty is through countryside – at least green agricultural fields that pass for countryside these days. This is what I saw;

There were two rabbits, one pheasant, one rat and a hedgehog. The crows were already at them. They will be cleared in an hour or so.

It does not sound a great number but that is on a twenty mile stretch in one day. I do not know how many hundreds of thousands of miles of road there are in Britain - probably millions but if you start multiplying that typical tally up over the miles and days it makes for grim reading.

If you start thinking of a similar picture over Europe, Africa, Australia and the rest of the world it is a heavy toll.

I do not greatly mourn the rabbits, rat or pigeon. They are the species that are plentiful. They have adapted and benefited from the environment we have created. I do mourn the hedgehog. That once plentiful animal is in decline.

Senseless death of the toads

When I was about twelve years old I used to go off collecting frogspawn every Spring with my mate Tony Hum. We couldn't wait for the weather to start improving so we could get back out there into the fields among the wild life. There was nothing we liked better than being up to our necks in mud hunting for a crested newt.

One of our favourite spots was a big pool next to the river Thames quite close to Walton Bridge. That was where the toads spawned. All the toads from the whole area congregated at that pool where they mated and festooned the reeds with their long strings of eggs. They were a sight to see. There is something magical about a large congregation of wild animals. The power of that instinct that pulls them back to this one spot to find a mate and spawn is transcendental. It is the same with whatever species, whether it is turtles coming back to a beach to lay their eggs or migratory birds all arriving in one lake after a flight of thousands of miles. There is an ethereal quality to it that sends a thrill down your spine.

We'd go there every year, stand and admire the wonderful sight, and collect a few of the hundreds of adults and a pail of toad spawn to take back and rear to little toadlets. It never failed to excite.

When we arrived at the spot we were stunned into shocked silence. It was like stumbling on the massacre after Culloden, the scene at the Alamo and the Battle of Hastings all rolled into one.

To start with there were heaps of dead toads piled up. There were toads crawling away as best they could with their hind legs hacked off. There were toads which had been inflated with straws, toads pinned to the ground with sticks through their bellies. The water was strewn with dead bodies which had been shot with air-gun pellets and catapults and had their bellies ripped open.

It was carnage.

There was not a living toad to be seen apart from the dying ones who were still writhing around.

Gradually our senses came back to us and the stunned shock was replaced by anger and fury. This was all recent. Whoever had done this couldn't be far away.

We dropped our things and raced off down the river bank to find them. There was blind madness in our heads.

Sure enough there was a gang of about a dozen older boys of around fourteen or fifteen years of age. They were sauntering along firing and sneering at the swans and ducks on the river. We charged at them with fists flying.

They punched us around a bit and threw us in the river and went off laughing.

We went back and got our things and silently went home.

We went back the next year, with desperate hope, but the pool was empty. Those boys had wiped out the entire toad population of the area in one fell swoop.

The Animal House

After college we went off around America for three months. We worked in restaurants and hitch-hiked round. We went up to Sequoia National Park to stare up at those colossal giants of trees that had been growing there for two and a half thousand years. That was hard to imagine. Through all of the history of Europe and back to Biblical times those trees had stood there. When Moses came down that mountain they were already hundreds of years old. When the Battle of Hastings raged they were already over one thousand five hundred years old. Early American Indians had walked under their canopies. They were impressive.

What was more astounding was the fact that some idiots with a chain-saw had taken it into their heads that it would be fun to ring those magnificent trees. They, probably in a drunken stupor, had gone and cut all round the trunks of some of the colossi. Cutting through the xylem and phloem and ensuring their death. It probably didn't even take long. A silly animal with a tool who has been alive for the blink of an eye could end the life of something that had lived that long in a matter of minutes. That about sums human beings up.

Some things make you ashamed to be human.

In the High Sierra we saw the oldest inhabitant of the planet. It was a scraggy bristle-cone pine, clinging into the crevice of a rock that was reputed to have been three thousand five hundred years old. It put your life in perspective. Imagine living for 3500 years! That's basically through the whole of human recorded history! If only trees could talk.

 When we returned in autumn 1971 the economic situation had worsened and I could not get casual work. Finally at Christmas I got work as a warehouseman at a central heating company warehouse. I worked there for six months to save the money to move back up to London.

In London I got work at my old college as a laboratory technician with day release to do a Master's degree. The pay was poor but we got by. The research was tedious. I investigated the biostratonomy of Lake Windermere through the identification of microfossil chironomid head capsules (midges). They are indicator organisms for oxygen levels in the lake. I was basically studying the way the lake silts up by peering down a microscope at segments of mud taken from a core from Lake Windermere. I had to tease out all the head capsules with a needle, identify them and work out the changes in species through time. It was boring and soul destroying.

I rapidly moved out of the laboratory stuff into the Animal House. This was good and bad. Bad because they used the animals for dissection and even vivisection and that meant I had to kill them and good because I got to work with lots of animals, care for them and make their life a bit nicer while they were alive.

Pete and I had both refused to continue with dissection when we were on our Zoology degree. We thought it was unethical unless you wanted to be a doctor or a vet where those skills might be required. We'd done it, seen it and did not need to keep doing it. Now I was the other side of the table, so to speak.

I found myself in charge of hundreds of rats, ten rabbits, forty guinea pigs and some fish. I had to breed them to maintain stock, clean them out three times a week and ensure they all had food and water. My other task was to pick up livestock from the station. This livestock consisted of live grass snakes, live salamanders and live frogs. These were live caught from Ireland and the continent and were used for dissection.

My first project was the rabbits and guinea pigs. The rabbits in particular were in need of assistance they were confined to these small cages where they sat on a grill that they shat and peed through. They could not even turn around. They sat and stared out, drank their water, ate their pellets and got fat. They were rarely used so some sat there for years moldering away in complete boredom. I aimed to do something about it.

I got some old wood and some zinc wire fencing and built a run. There was a little grassy patch at the side of the Animal House. I fenced it off. I put the big fat lollopy rabbits out in it. At first they sat there not quite believing it. They had never seen daylight, felt the ground beneath their feet or smelt fresh air. Then they relaxed, began to nibble the grass and shuffled around. Before long they were running, bucking and shagging each other with great gusto and delight. It was heart-warming to see.

I then put the guinea pigs out in the run and they had fun running about chuntering at each other.

All was well.

I was planning what to do with the rats. They were grouped in batches in cages and at least had company and could move around so they weren't quite so pressing but I had plans to build a big multilayered cage with ladders and ropes that they would have loved. The rats were beautiful. I handled them all three times a week when I cleaned them out and I never got bitten once. I would grab a handful of four or five rats and plonk them in a bucket while I cleaned the cage and then I plonked them back. No problem.

Then there was trouble. Somebody had spragged.

I got a deputation from management. They came and inspected my rabbit run, ignored me, and made various hmmmpphhing noises. Later that week I got a formal letter telling me to take the run down. Seemingly it was against Animal House protocol. The animals had to be kept in sterile conditions to ensure standardisation. I was behaving illegally.

I was furious.

Undeterred I set up a run in the backroom and let them out there. It wasn't as good but it would do.

My second strategy was to name the animals. When a technician came for a guinea pig for an experiment I gave them a named animal. This is Justine I'd say, passing her over. Immediately you named them you seemingly gave them a personality and I had technicians in tears.

I received my second formal warning.

I was becoming increasingly disturbed. The live caught animals were arriving dead. Over half were always dead on arrival. It was seemingly normal. They over-ordered to compensate. It meant that I was emptying boxes of frogs from Ireland packed with damp moss and piling up dead frogs in a heap on the floor. I got a sizeable mound of dead frogs so I took some photos. I did not have anything in mind I merely thought it should be recorded as management did not seem concerned. It was particularly distressing with the salamanders which came from Spain and I knew were on the endangered list. Not so many of them died but I felt they should never have been live caught and used for dissection in the first place.

Even worse was the way they killed them for dissection. They were put in a freezer and frozen live. On occasion they were thawed out and came back to life with half their body frozen solid. It was distressing.

Nobody took any notice of my complaints.

The last straw was the cats. The Psychology Department did vivisection experiments on cats for their students. One experiment involved drugging a cat, slicing its skull open and cutting into its brain to demonstrate what the various regions did. Another involved injecting the live cats, strung up on clamps and retort stands, with various drugs to see their reactions.

I took exception to these experiments. The cats were beautiful long-haired Persians with very friendly dispositions. I spent ages sitting in their run petting them. They were very affectionate. I argued with the Psychologists that there was no need for these repeated experiments. They could film the thing and show their students. There was no need to sacrifice the cats in this way. They did not agree.

I went in and took shots of the cats being subject to this vivisection.

I was promptly served with a Home Office writ. Seemingly I had signed some official document. If I released those photos I would be prosecuted and jailed.

It was a short career as an Animal House technician. I left to go into teaching.

The Natural History Museum

When I was nine and ten I had a friend called Billy. He was a bit eccentric and precocious. We used to go on fossil hunts together. He always wanted to find the Latin names of our specimens and label them.

I remember one day we were looking for fossils among the limestone in an old quarry when a university team turned up. One of them asked us if we'd found anything and this nine year old Billy told him - 'nothing much - just a pile of brachiopods, lamellibranches and echinoderms. We have yet to name the species.' The guy was bowled over.

Billy and I used to regularly go up to the Natural History museum by train from Walton on Thames on our own. We'd spend the day doing a section. One week it would be the fossils; the next week the minerals and then all the stuffed animals. The place was still quite staid and very much an old Victorian collection that was not put together in the way modern museums are but we loved it.

I was always impressed by the stuffed Dodo and often went to peer at it. It symbolised the stupidity and cruelty of sailors. The Dodos were so docile that the sailors just clubbed them all to death to eat. They wiped out every last one. Life was cruel and those sailors were heartless. They would catch live turtles and place them in deck on their backs so that they would have live meat to eat later in the voyage. There was never a thought for the distress of the animals.

One day we were up there looking at a display of the contents of a penguin's stomach. This gentleman started asking us questioned and we explained what the various stones were for and why the penguins ate them. He was impressed and took us along to the canteen and bought us a bottle of pop and cake.

We went home and told our parents and how we arranged to meet up next week and that was the end of our visits to the Natural History Museum. They obviously thought he was a paedophile! (On the other hand it could have been David Attenborough!). It could have been my connection to a different life! Ho hum.

Yellowstone Park

We've been to Yellowstone Park twice. You'd never know from looking at its placid exterior that it is a potential world-changing catastrophe in the making. Yellowstone is a massive caldera of a volcano that is poised to collapse and spark an eruption that could be of a size to cover half of America in lava and cause a long long winter and probably a mini-ice-age due to the atmospheric ash.

There's not a lot we can do about it at present so perhaps it is best to just focus on the good stuff. It is a place of beauty, tranquility and a haven for wild life.

We found black bears, moose, elk and bison roaming freely in the forests and meadows. There were chipmunks in the trees and marmots in the rocks.

The natural hot springs with their multicoloured tiers of mineral deposits stained with metallic ores and hot-spring bacteria and algae are beautiful and its great geysers spouting up from the molten rock below are a marvel.

Places like Yellowstone Park fill you with hope for the future.

Mr. Davies the Biologist and Mr. Tranter the Rural Scientist

Some people you can emphathise with even if they never know. Mr. Tranter and Mr. Davies were two of them. I often think that we do not tell the people who have touched us and changed us how much they meant to us anywhere near enough. These two teachers had a long lasting effect on me and my life. They changed me and I now belatedly thank them.

Mr. Davies was an old teacher coming to the end of his career. He taught me Biology for one short year. He was a kind and gentle man.

I remember him coming down the corridor and stopping to talk to me. I had my locker open and it was stuffed with milk bottles of water into which I'd put twigs of food plants with my caterpillar haul for that lunch-time. His face lit up with delight as he asked me about the various caterpillars and beamed with enjoyment as we shared our enthusiasm for the creatures. It doesn't take much to transmit your love of nature. He radiated it in spades.

On the other hand Mr. Tranter was a young lively teacher who joined us for one short year. I do not remember even talking to him, though I know I did, but I do remember his enthusiasm and idealism. He was an inspiring young man. He spoke to us about living sustainably in a hut on Box Hill with his own vegetable patch and chickens. It sounded idyllic to me though I remember everyone else thought he was nuts. I was bowled over with the idea of living simply and sustainably.

Mr. Tranter was taking a course in navigation and, along with a friend, was building his own boat to head off round the world.

I hope he made it and had a brilliant time. I hope he is presently living somewhere nice in the countryside after a long fulfilling life, still vibrant in his mid-seventies and full of that zest for life. - Thanks guys.

Nuclear dumps

One major problem with the nuclear industry is the difficulty of getting rid of the nuclear waste. It remains dangerous for hundreds of thousands of years. The half-life of uranium is 4.7 billion years. That means that if you were to put a ton of it into the ground in 4.7 billion years time you'd still have half a ton of the stuff.

That doesn't sound good to me.

It makes you wonder what British Nuclear Fuels were thinking when they were dumping that stuff off the sides of ships into shallow water in concrete lined barrels that degrade in double quick time. Were they stupid or thoughtless?

In my opinion there is only one way to deal with nuclear waste. It needs vitrifying into glass cubes and storing deep underground in specially prepared chambers in rock that is stable and not subject to seismic activity. I know that is expensive but that price needs building in to the overall plan. Nuclear power is not the cheap option they would have us believe.

So when the government proposed a cheap plan to set up a nuclear dump on the site of a disused power station on the South Bank of the Humber I opposed it. I did not think that it was safe to put high level radio-active waste in barrels in a concrete lined dump on land. In my opinion concrete does not last thousands of years. Radio-active material would leak and contaminate groundwater. That is precisely what has happened in next to no time in America with similar projects.

Doing things on the cheap is not a viable alternative. It causes huge long-term problems and ends up costing a great deal more to clear up the mess.

So I went on a march through Hull carrying my banner. I did not take my kids because they were not yet old enough to make up their own mind and I do not believe in indoctrination.

Shortly after that protest march a man knocked on my door with a poster advertising a public meeting in the town library regarding the nuclear dump. He asked if I was going and could I display the poster. I readily agreed to both.

On the night of the meeting I went along to the library. I was expecting a big turn-out so I was a bit surprised to find I could park directly outside. I went in expecting the meeting to be in the main hall and was directed down to a dingy little basement room. It was very quiet.

When I went into the room there were only five people in there but they were delighted to see me and welcomed me in. We had a great chat about the wrongs of nuclear dumping. They were extremely friendly and did not seem too extreme to me. There was no talk of insurrection and mayhem. But seemingly they were a small ultra-left wing group. They just seemed like nice concerned guys.

The following week my phone was tapped. There was a click when I picked the receiver up and when my friends called their calls were intercepted and they were questioned as to who they were and who they were after and why.

That caused a bit of a stir with them and me. I took to picking up the phone and having conversations with the invisible people at the other end of the line.

When I rang the telephone people they assured me it was nothing sinister the interceptions were merely to check nuisance calls.

Louisiana Swamps

Because my daughter and her family lived in Baton Rouge for a few years we were fortunate enough to get to go to stay and explore both Louisiana and Mississippi. It enabled me to indulge two of my life-time obsessions: the Mississippi Delta Blues and the environment of the Louisiana swamps.

The Louisiana swamps and bayous are a unique environment. The first swamp I went near was at dusk and I was immediately met with a swarm of mosquitoes and got bitten to pieces. But it was a wondrous sight and it was worth it.

We later walked round the swamps at a reasonable time of day and avoided the attention of mosquito swarms. We were able to see the many snakes, golden orb spiders and the cypress trees with their winged buttresses for support and their pointed knees sticking up out of the water. The water was green with weed and the trees were festooned with Spanish Moss that gave it an eerie unreal atmosphere. It was a very different type of place to anything I'd ever seen before.

We took a boat trip out round the bayous and saw the alligators and herons up close. I even got to hold a fair sized three foot alligator and I can report that they are exceedingly heavy. I don't know how they manage to float. It was extremely placid and long suffering and put up with being handled without struggling or trying to bite me.

The bayous were extremely atmospheric with their green water coated in weed, the cypress trees with their great buttresses in the water all hanging with Spanish Moss and great birds standing on the branches or wading in the shallows fishing, more so than the swamps. I can see why they use them as the backdrop to a number of films. It was a special environment to live in.

Australia and the Ozone layer

There was much concern back in the 1990s when it was discovered that there was a hole in the ozone layer over the Antarctic. Around the Earth there is a thin layer of Ozone up there in the stratosphere that is constantly ionizing and breaking up and reforming. This layer is responsible for filtering out a lot of the sun's Ultra-Violet light. Without it the UV levels go through the roof and are damaging to plants and animals. They are particularly harmful to humans because of our naked skin and white people in particular who are lacking in protective melanin.

The concern was that this hole would spread, the protective ozone would thin and we'd all be subject to the UV radiation which would result in cataracts, cancer and damage to crops reducing their yield.

Fortunately they discovered what was causing it. It was the CFC - chlorofluorocarbons - used in for example - polystyrene packaging and refrigerator cooling fluids.

Legislation was passed and the use of CFCs regulated. The CFCs were cleared up and it appears that the ozone layer is repairing itself.

That is a positive outcome and a great success story!

However UV light is still a major problem in places like Australia where the sun is strong and there is a real outdoor life-style. The incidence of melanoma is high. They have adopted a 'Slip, Slap, Slop' policy which is almost universally adhered to and has proved very effective at reducing cancer rates - Slip on a T-shirt, Slap on a hat and Slop on some sunscreen!

Travelling around Scotland

Pete and Trudy came across for a planned trip up to Scotland and out to the Orkneys. We planned to take in the splendors of the Scottish countryside and brave the midges. I also wanted to see all the Neolithic sites, like Scara Brae, the Stenness Stones and the Ring of Brodgar.

The further North we went the more spectacular the scenery. Glen Nevis was incredible with its towering mountains, trees and waterfall. The highlands were all magnificent.

We walked round the lakes and saw the ever-present oyster catchers with their red beaks and feet, seals basking on the rocks and curlews in the fields. We even came across some otter spraint but no otters, pine martins or golden eagles.

We did get to see ospreys over the lakes and nesting at the osprey centre and red squirrels who were brilliantly delightful.

On the boat out to the Orkneys we looked for Orcas. They had been around the week before but must have known we were coming but in the great loch we got to see dolphins at play.

That made my day.

Fracking, the Seven Estuary Barrier, Nuclear Power and Wind Farms

There is a debate going on as to where we should get our energy from. It seems to me that many people and groups are opposed to everything and that seems unrealistic.

They do not want wind farms because they think they are unsightly and cause damage to birds.

They don't want fracking because of the use of chemicals that might get into the water supply along with escaping gas.

They don't want gas and coal because of the Acid Rain and Carbon.

They don't want nuclear because of the dangers of a melt-down and the problems over getting rid of the waste.

They don't want a Seven Estuary Barrier because of the potential damage to the mud-flats that are an essential stop for migrating birds.

I can understand all these arguments. Ideally I am in support of all forms of green energy that produces electricity through non-polluting methods. I have nothing against wind-farms on land but particularly like the off-shore versions as I think the structures will provide great benefits to marine life. All kinds of seaweed and invertebrates attach to the structures as we have seen around oil rigs, and they attract in fish. They become sanctuaries for sea life of all descriptions.

I also think we should look into wave and solar power and insulate our houses better. I applaud the government initiative to make our houses more energy efficient with insulation, double glazing and cavity wall insulation. I just wish we had legislation as tight as Scandinavian countries with triple glazing, heat retrieval systems and extra insulation. That would cut the need for energy.

Hydroelectric is clean. The Seven Estuary may well be a long-term solution (If incredibly costly) if we can find a way of protecting the wetlands.

In the meantime I would prefer we took gas from fracking rather than burning coal or oil or importing gas from Russia.

I do not think nuclear is a safe option. Japan is getting rid of all its nuclear power. They have decided following the aftermath of the Tsunami that it is simply too unsafe.

It is no good being opposed to everything. We have to choose between a lot of unpleasant choices.

That means selecting the best of the bunch.

The answer lies in the numbers. Reduce your population and you reduce your energy needs, carbon footprint, and pollution. That is the priority.

Decline of wild life in Britain in my life-time

There is no doubt that I have witnessed a tremendous decline in wild-life in Britain over the last fifty years. The rich environment of my youth is gone. The meadows are no longer crawling with insects and arachnids, buzzing with bees and alive with bobbing, dancing butterflies.

I look in the ditches as I pass and they appear largely devoid of life.

I look in the willow and sallow and no longer find the eye-hawks, poplar hawks or puss-moths. I check the privet hedges and have yet to find any privet hawk moths.

My car is no longer festooned with dead bugs when I drive around.

I lift any piece of corrugated iron I come across and do not find the grass snakes and slow-worms that used to be there.

I look at the huge new housing estates, the new roads, the encroachment into the once hallowed green-belt and all I see is nature on the retreat.

My travels round the world have furnished me with even more stark and disturbing images.

There are too many of us. We are impacting too much. We are destroying the ecosystem of our planet.

We need to address it urgently. I want my grandchildren to see all the wondrous sights I have seen.

I do not see this as all doom and gloom; I see it as a clarion call to face up to what is happening around the world and do something about it.

This is my little bit.

Solutions

The solutions to the environmental catastrophe are essentially simple. They are things such as the need to:

- Reduce human populations to a sustainable 4 billion

- Use efficient green technology that reduces toxic pollution and greenhouse gasses.

- Ensure that at least 50% of the world is set aside for wilderness environments – including a range of all different habitats.

- Protect rainforest environments

- Make all fishing, logging, mining and food production sustainable and not destructive to the environment

- Prevent pollution of land, sea, fresh water and air

- Prevent hunting and poaching in wilderness areas

- Ensure all human beings have a reasonable standard of living so that they do not need to kill wild-life, destroy wilderness and encroach on other creatures

- Value all life and the rich tapestry of creatures and plants that constitute a healthy ecosystem

- Increase spending on monitoring the environment and research into superior green technology

- Increase spending into research to negate global catastrophes such as viruses, comets, volcanic activity, earthquake and tsunami

- Educate people to live in harmony with the planet in a sustainable manner

- Counter superstition and ignorant religious beliefs that support the use of exotic animal parts in medicine, the creation of large families and the rape of the planet.

That is all.

The theory is simple but the pragmatics of putting that theory in place is difficult. It requires thinking on a global scale, clear legislation to encourage development of superior technology, clear legislation to ensure the environment is respected and policies that create greater equality, education and higher standards of living.

Global thinking requires the power of a whole-world organization such as the United Nations. Only when we have risen above the petty interests of nations can we establish effective mechanisms for dealing with the problems of overpopulation, conservation and pollution.

It is crazy that France gives incentives for couples to have large families and Islam and Catholicism promote large families when the global population is out of control. It is counterproductive to protect the breeding grounds of songbirds in Africa if those same birds are remorselessly hunted in Spain and France when they migrate. It is pointless for European countries to have laws on marine pollution if South Africa is dumping millions of tons of raw sewage from its townships straight into the ocean and Peru empties its refuse from Lima on the seashore.

We have to have a unified international set of rules and regulations.

We have to raise up the standard of living of Third World countries so that they do not have to eat everything that moves and do not need large families because of high infant mortality and to support them through old age and illness.

There is nothing esoteric about solving these problems. What stands in our way is greed, selfishness, expansion, growth, corruption, ignorance and exploitation.

I would like to believe that we can develop the will to live sustainably in harmony with all life on this jewel of a planet before it is too late. We are in danger of losing our rainforests, wilderness and ocean fauna. I would hope we could step back from the brink before all those precious species are eradicated from the wild.

There are a multitude of excellent initiatives already taking place. A lot more needs doing.

I urge everyone to help save a tiger, whale, rhino, gorilla, chimp, dolphin and elephant and thousands of others from being killed. They are being hunted, harpooned and shot and their habitat is being relentlessly destroyed. What a loss! And what an indictment of humanity!

The environment can be saved. It is perfectly achievable.

I would love those intelligent beings in the distant future to be looking at a rich and exceedingly thick band of rock, full of varied fossils, that represents the splendor of the Anthropocene.

I would like my next book on the environment to be called – 'The Anthropocene – from the jaws of Apocalypse into the heights of glory'.